Child: New and Selected Poems 1991–2011

MIMI KHALVATI was born in Tehran and grew up on the Isle of Wight. She attended Drama Centre London and worked as a theatre director in London and in Tehran. She is the founder of The Poetry School where she now teaches. Carcanet publish her six previous collections, including *In White Ink* (1991), *Mirrorwork* (1995), *Entries on Light* (1997), *The Chine* (2002) and *The Meanest Flower* (2007), which was a Poetry Book Society Recommendation and shortlisted for the T.S. Eliot Prize. She received a Cholmondely Award in 2006 and is a Fellow of the Royal Society of Literature.

T0288209

Also by Mimi Khalvati from Carcanet Press

In White Ink
Mirrorwork
Entries on Light
Selected Poems
The Chine
The Meanest Flower

MIMI KHALVATI

Child

New and Selected Poems
1991–2011

CARCANET

First published in Great Britain in 2011 by
Carcanet Press Limited
Alliance House
Cross Street
Manchester M2 7AQ

www.carcanet.co.uk

A CIP catalogue record for this book is available from the British Library
ISBN 978 1 84777 094 3

The publisher acknowledges financial assistance from Arts Council England

Supported by
ARTS COUNCIL
ENGLAND

Typeset by XL Publishing Services, Tiverton
Printed and bound in England by SRP Ltd, Exeter

For my grandchildren

Besan and Kai

Acknowledgements

Acknowledgements are due to the editors of the following publications in which these poems have appeared:

'Iowa Daybook' was written during a fellowship at the International Writers Program in Iowa in 2006. A longer version was published online in the *International Literary Quarterly*, Issue 2, February 2008.

'The Streets of La Roue' was commissioned by Het beschrijf and first published in a Dutch translation in *Vers Brussel, Poëzie in de stad* by Het beschrijf/Uitgeverij Vrijdag (Brussels, 2009). It also appeared in *This Life on Earth* (Sea of Faith (SOF) Network (UK), 2009).

'Afterword', an elegy for Archie Markham, was published by *Staple* and in *The Forward Book of Poetry 2010*. An Italian translation by Eleonora Chiavetta appeared in *Poeti e Poesia* (Pagine, 2011).

'Night Sounds' was published in *Poetry Review* and in *A Shadow on the Wall* (Soaring Penguin, 2011).

'River Sounding' was commissioned by Romesh Gunesekara during his residency at Somerset House as a response to Bill Fontana's eponymous sound installation. The sequence appeared in *The Long Poem Magazine* and an extract, 'I never remember my dreams', in *The North*.

'The Poet's House' was published in *Entailing Happiness*, a festschrift for Robert Vas Dias (Infinity Press, 2010). It was written at Almassera Vella, where Christopher North runs writing courses, and appears on their website www.oldolivepress.com.

I am extremely grateful to Arts Council England for granting me a writing award in 2009. And warm thanks are due to Jane Duran for responding to the manuscript with such care, Myra Schneider and her group; Aamer Hussein, Jacqueline Gabbitas, Martin Parker, Marilyn Hacker and Alfred Corn for their friendship and support.

Contents

SELECTED POEMS

I

II

III

from Entries on Light

IV

NEW AND UNCOLLECTED POEMS

SELECTED POEMS

I

Shanklin Chine

It surfaces at moments, unlooked-for,
when the little crooked child appears
to bar your way: demanding no crooked
sixpence as she stands behind the stile
in her little gingham frock and the blood
she has in mind drawn behind her gaze.

Are you the guardian of the Chine?
(Perhaps she needs some recognition.)
Of course she never talks.
She only has the one face – dark and solemn,
the one stance – blackboard-set
and a wit as nimble as the Chine

stopping short at forgiveness
that could only come with time or power
or a body large enough to fit her brain.
Is there something I could give her?
Some blow to crack her ice?
Human warmth to make her feel the same?

Genie of the Chine, she reappears at moments
when I am closest to waterways, underworlds,
little crooked streams through lichen
and liverwort that end so prematurely –
though *she* is there, like Peter Pan,
or the barbed-wire children who bang tin cans

or the child you would have loved
like any mother, any father, had you been
an adult, not the child with no demands
for sixpences in puddings, pumpkins
on the table or any pumpkin pies gracing
homes that had you standing at their gates.

Genie of the Chine, she reappears
from time to time, when I am closest to myself.

Writing Home

As far back as I remember, 'home'
had an empty ring. Not hollow, but visual
like a place ringed on a map, monochrome
in a white disc. Around it were the usual
laurel hedges, the chine, the hockey pitch,
the bridge. On one side, the crab-apple tree
with its round seat, whose name puzzled me, which
wasn't surprising since everyone but me
seemed to understand such things, take for granted
apples can't be eaten, crabs can be planted.

Writing home meant writing in that ring, mostly
to Mummy. Mummy had a white fur coat
and framed in it her face looked tired and ghostly.
I am very well and happy, I wrote,
meaning it. Sensing somewhere in that frame
a face too far away, too lost, to worry.
And why would I? Worry should keep, like shame,
its head down in dreams. Sorry sorry sorry
I can't write anymore goodbye love Mimi
I wrote after only four lines to Mummy.

There's no irony in that. I was six.
Right from the start, home was an empty space
I sent words to. Mapped my world, tried to fix
meanings to it. Not for me, but to trace
highlights someone could follow: Brownies, Thinking
Day, films, a fathers' hockey match, a play
called Fairy Slippers, picnics, fire drills, swimming.
Even the death of a King. When my birthday?
I wrote at the same time, dropping the 'is',
too proud of my new question mark to notice.

My mother kept all my letters for ten years,
then gave them back to me. Perhaps they never
touched her, were intended only for my ears
for I never knew her then or asked whether
she made sense of them, if my references
to the small world of a girls' school in England
had any meaning. It was the fifties. Suez,
Mossadegh, white cardies, Clarks sandals. And,
under the crab-apple tree, taking root,
words in a mouth puckered from wild, sour fruit.

The Alder Leaf

It is perfect. And of a green so bright
no other green has a say in it, fine-veined
and tiny-toothed, in short, a leaf a child might
choose to love, remember. And later, name.
Children love what is perfect, the best catkin,
blossom with each whisker in place. But sometimes
on a path they will halt and bend to a matted
object strangely furred, spun with gauze but numb
to prodding and hard as rock, neither insect
nor larva, stone nor egg and troubled both
by choosing and ignoring it or failing
to find something on a nature trail, loath
to ask but asking, *what is it?* learn nothing
of shit too late to name in retrospect.

Writing Letters

After chapel on Sundays we wrote letters,
ruling pencil lines on airmails. Addresses
on front and back often bearing the same name,
same initial even, for in some countries
they don't bother to draw fine lines between
family members with an alphabet.

Those who remembered their first alphabet
covered the page in reams of squiggly letters
while those who didn't envied them. Between
them was the fine line of having addresses
that spelt home, home having the ring of countries
still warm on the tongue, still ringing with their name,

and having addresses gone cold as a name
no one could pronounce in an alphabet
with no *k-h*. Some of us left our countries
behind where we left our names. Wrote our letters
to figments of imagination: addresses
to darlings, dears, we tried to tell between,

guessing at norms, knowing the choice between
warmth and reserve would be made in the name
of loyalty. As we learnt our addresses
off by heart, the heart learnt an alphabet
of doors, squares, streets off streets, where children's letters
felt as foreign as ours from foreign countries.

Countries we revisited later; countries
we reclaimed, disowned again, caught between
two alphabets, the back and front of letters.
Street names change; change loyalties: a king's name
for a saint's. Even the heart's alphabet
needs realignment when the old addresses

sink under flyovers and new addresses
never make it into books where their countries
are taken as read. In an alphabet
of silence, dust, where the distance between
darling and dear is desert, where no name
is traced in the sand, no hand writes love letters,

none of my addresses can tell between
camp and home, neither of my countries name
this alphabet a cause for writing letters.

Villanelle

No one is there for you. Don't call, don't cry.
No one is in. No flurry in the air.
Outside your room are floors and doors and sky.

Clocks speeded, slowed, not for you to question why,
tick on. Trust them. Be good, behave. Don't stare.
No one is there for you. Don't call, don't cry.

Cries have their echoes, echoes only fly
back to their pillows, flocking back from where
outside your room are floors and doors and sky.

Imagine daylight. Daylight doesn't lie.
Fool with your shadows. Tell you nothing's there,
no one is there for you. Don't call, don't cry.

But daylight doesn't last. Today's came by
to teach you the dimensions of despair.
Outside your room are floors and doors and sky.

Learn, when in turn they turn to you, to sigh
and say: You're right, I know, life isn't fair.
No one is there for you. Don't call, don't cry.
Outside your room are floors and doors and sky.

Sadness

It is difficult to know what to do with so much happiness
Naomi Shihab Nye

With sadness there is something to rub against –
these, your words, for unhappiness is speechless.
Sad air breathes, at whatever altitude,
recirculating air. Rub it against glass

and the shape it takes is nothing but the melt
of breath. Follow it with your eyes along
the patterns of the curtains and it will trap you
in a leit-motif you can't escape. You're wrong.

When the world falls in around you, there are
no wounds to tend, holes to fill, no prop
of stubborn plaster; tenements don't crumble.
I've measured the ceiling for the curtain's drop,

metres are where I left them. *When the world*
falls in around you, you have pieces to pick up,
something to hold in your hands you say. Like this?
this button? A grey that fell, just now, a trick

of heaven? No, it comes from my green pyjamas.
Happiness sews on buttons. Sadness looks for
sadness to couple with, not comfort. The minute
I lift my head from the page, my heart takes over.

Listening to Strawberry

for Aubrey ('Strawberry') de Selincourt

I knew it as the poetry I could never hear
without his voice to give it utterance
and the way it ran inside me was clearer,
closer, than the way it ran in others

though they loved it too, owned it too
but owning so much else, loved it that much less.
Owning so little now, I recall how he drew
it out with pipesmoke, through long crossed legs

out of the earth as if he, so long and lean,
were a brook for the vowels to run through,
knocking consonants like little stones
to quaver in their wake. Certainty can quaver too.

And still retain its faith. Outcast
in its deepest spells of orphanhood, the soul
can recall – through memories of grass
and place, a shaking hand on a pipe's bowl

that indicates a turn of phrase – an undertow
to weather, a companionship that being human,
echoing high in leafy woods, confiding low
when at our lowest, deprived of human company,

makes deprivation sweet to bear. And for
those of us who heard him, in our girlhoods
when girlhood was still a word to stand for
a kind of kingdom, a wreath around our heads,

it was a binding that netted us together
like wild strawberries never safe from bird
or hand; a murmur I can still remember
with or without remembering the words.

The Chine

To be back on the island is to be
cast adrift but always facing the same
mother who stays ashore, is always there
despite the mist. My balcony's a crib.
Through its bars the waves rush in. Not a ship,
not a gull, and the sky in its slow revolve
winding the Isle of Wight with a giant key.

We are spinning backwards in a slow spin;
we are in a time warp, a gap, a yawn,
a chine that cleaves the mind in two, a line
on the land's belly. Shanklin. Rhylstone Gardens
where an old man rolls tobacco, as sparing
with the strands as the years have been with him.
Luccombe with its own chine, barely a stream.

Every childhood has its chine, upper world
and lower. Time itself seems vertical
and its name too implies both bank and stream.
To be back on the island is to walk
in both worlds at the same time, looking down
on talus, horsehair fern notched through the Ice Age,
Stone Age, Bronze Age and still here at our heels;

looking up like an elf, ears cocked to silence,
from a zigzag of silver and silt. A chine
is a form of urgency to reach the sea.
As coastlines have eroded, chines, like orphans
stranded in a high place without their slope
of history, have had to take a short cut,
make deep cuts into the soft clay of cliffs.

Childhood has its railings too. And its catches
of glove on rust, twisted wire with a slight give.
Playthings. For in an upper world that turns
beachfronts into toytowns, patches of moss
into stands of minuscule trees, no railing
is not a harp, no rung a wind might play on
something other than its maker intended.

But in the lower world we dream. We listen.
Not for water which is the sound of listening
or for schoolgirls passing above unseen.
Under lawns, hotels, we sit hours midstream,
crouched under a hundred blankets. If eyes
were ears, we'd hear the very mud-bed thicken,
rise in little mounds where the water's clean.

Every path brings us back to the beginning.
Shanklin Chine is closed for the winter, both ends
barred with notices. But the mind is not.
Or memory. And time is spinning backwards
with the mainland out of sight and the great plain
where herds roamed the floor of the English Channel
and were drowned by it flush again with valleys.

I look down on them, my own that were fed
by chines, from the long esplanade of light
on Keats Green and seem to remember walking
with my mother here, running my hand on railings.
The beautiful inn on the corner's a wreck
and there, at the bend, where the light's so bright
and people walking down the steep incline

pause at the top before walking down, black
against the blaze before their torsos sink,
something vanishes, there, where the path drops
and a young boy comes running down the hill.
Never, O God, to be afraid of love
is inscribed on a new bench where I sit,
facing the headland with its crown in mist.

Nostalgia

It's a night for nostalgia he said.
I felt I was missing something, some
echo of nights we must have shared
in separate alleyways, far off home

rain drew him back to, or clouds,
or the particular light behind rain.
I was nostalgic for words, last words
of a poem I would read on the train.

There was a power cut today. I lit
three candles, ate lamb and read
by candlelight. The beauty of it
was too lonely so I went to bed.

It rained then. In the daylight dark.
I lay there till I heard a click
and voices. When the lights came back
it was like a conjuring trick –

there they were, the animated creatures
of my life I had thought inanimate
objects. And I was the one conjured
out of their dream of a dark planet.

Earls Court

I brush my teeth harder when the gum bleeds.
Arrive alone at parties, leaving early.

The tide comes in, dragging my stare
from pastures I could call my own.

Through the scratches on the record – *Ah! Vieni, vieni!* –
I concentrate on loving.

I use my key. No duplicate of this.
Arrive alone at parties, leaving early.

I brush my teeth harder when the gum bleeds.
Sing to the fern in the steam. Not even looking –

commuters buying oranges, Italian vegetables,
bucket flowers from shores I might have danced in, briefly.

I use my key – a lost belonging on the stair.
Sing to the fern in the steam. I wash my hair.

The tide goes out, goes out. The body's wear and tear.
Commuters' faces turn towards me: bucket flowers.

A man sits eyeing destinations on the train.
He wears Islamic stubble, expensive clothes, two rings.

He talks to himself in Farsi, loudly like a drunk.
Laughs aloud to think where life has brought him.

Eyeing destinations on the train – a lost belonging –
talks to himself with a laugh I could call my own.

Like a drunk I want to neighbour him, sit beside
his stubble's scratch, turn his talking into chatting.

I want to tell him I have a ring like his,
only smaller. I want to see him use his key.

I want to hear the child who runs to him call
Baba! I want to hear him answer, turning

from his hanging coat: *Beeya, Babajune, beeya!*
Ah! Vieni, vieni!…

Baba Mostafa

He circles slowly and the walls of the room,
this Maryland cocoon, swirl as though the years
were not years but faces and he, at eighty,
in his warm woolly robe, were the last slow waltz.

'Children,' he would say, '*truly* love me!
And I have always, always loved children.'
'It's true,' she'd say, coming through the arch.
'Sarajune, you love Baba Mostafa, don't you?
D'you love Baba Mostafa or Maman Guity, hah?
Here, eat this.' 'For God's sake, woman,
do you want her to choke! Come, Sarajune, dance...
da-dum, da-dum, da-dum, da-da...'

He circles slowly, the child on his shoulder
nestled like a violin and the ruches of a smile
on the corners of his lips as though the babygro'
beneath his hand were glissades of satin.

'*Wunderschön! Das ist wunderschön!*' He lingers
on the umlaut he learned as a student on a scholarship
from Reza Shah and on the lips of a Fräulein
whose embouchure lives on in him, takes him back
through all those years, through marriages, children,
reversals of fortune, remembering how in wartime
foodstuffs left his home for hers – manna from Isfahan,
sweetmeats from Yazd, dried fruit from Azarbaijan.

He circles slowly, on paisley whorls
that once were cypress-trees bowing to the wind,
as though these 'perfect moslems' were reflections
of his coat-tails lifting on a breeze from the floor.

'I swear to God,' he blubbered, only days before
his laryngotomy, 'I was a good man. I never stole.
And if – and who can say? – you never had the father
my other children had, God knows it wasn't in my hands.'

'How is he?' they whispered in doorways as I buried
my butt-ends in beds of azaleas. Months later,
he writes: 'I can't eat *gut* and sleep *gut*.' He never could:
holding up *Der Spiegel*, in the small hours, to the lamp.

And now he circles, from room to room,
with a grandchild for company who step by step
outstrips him as he learns – re-learns – to talk…
da-dum, da-dum, da-dum, da-da…

Coma

Mr Khalvati? Larger than life he was;
too large to die so they wired him up on a bed.
Small as a soul he is on the mountain ledge.

Lids gone thin as a babe's. If it's mist he sees
it's no mist he knows by name. *Can you hear me,
Mr Khalvati?* Larger than life he was

and the death he dies large as the hands that once
drowned mine and the salt of his laugh in the wave.
Small as a soul he is on the mountain ledge.

Can you squeeze my hand? (Ach! Where are the hands
I held in mine to pull me back to the baize?)
Mr Khalvati? Larger than life he was

with these outstretched hands that squeezing squeeze
thin air. Wired he is, tired he is and there,
small as a soul he is on the mountain ledge.

No nudging him out of the nest. No one to help him
fall or fly, there's no coming back to the baize.
Mr Khalvati? Larger than life he was.
Small as a soul he is on the mountain ledge.

The Bowl

The path begins to climb the hills that confine the lake-basin. The ascent is steep and joyless; but it is as nothing compared with the descent on the other side, which is long, precipitous, and inconceivably nasty. This is the famous Kotal-i-Pir-i-Zan, or Pass of the Old Woman.

Some writers have wondered at the origin of the name. I feel no such surprise... For, in Persia, if one aspired, by the aid of a local metaphor, to express anything that was peculiarly uninviting, timeworn, and repulsive, a Persian old woman would be the first and most forcible simile to suggest itself. I saw many hundreds of old women... in that country... and I crossed the Kotal-i-Pir-i-Zan, and I can honestly say that whatever derogatory or insulting remarks the most copious of vocabularies might be capable of expending upon the one, could be transferred, with equal justice, to the other.

...At the end of the valley the track... discloses a steep and hideous descent, known to fame, or infamy, as the Kotal-i-Dokhter, or Pass of the Maiden.

...As I descended the Daughter, and alternately compared and contrasted her features with those of the Old Woman, I fear that I irreverently paraphrased a well-known line,

O matre laeda filia laedior!

George Nathaniel Curzon, *Persia and the Persian Question* (1892)

i

The bowl is big and blue. A flash of leaf
along its rim is green, spring-green, lime
and herringbone. Across the glaze where fish swim,
over the loose-knit waves in hopscotch-black,
borders of fish-eye and cross-stitch, chestnut trees
throw shadows: candles, catafalques and barques
and lord knows what, what ghost of ancient seacraft,
what river-going name we give to shadows.

Inside the bowl where clay has long since crusted,
under the dust and loam, leaf forms lie
fossilized. They have come from mountain passes,
orchards where no water runs, stony tracks
with only threadbare shade for mares and mule foals.
They are named: cuneiform and ensiform,
spathulate and sagittate and their margins
are serrated, lapidary, lobed.

My book of botany is green: the gloss
of coachpaint, carriages, Babushka dolls,
the clouded genie jars of long ago.
Inside my bowl a womb of air revolves.
What tadpole of the margins, holly-spine
of seahorse could be nosing at its shallows,
what honeycomb of sunlight, marbled green
of malachite be cobbled in its hoop?

I squat, I stoop. My knees are either side
of bowl. My hands are eyes around its crescent.
The surface of its story feathers me,
my ears are wrung with rumour. On a skyline
I cannot see a silhouette carves vase-shapes
into sky: baby, belly, breast, thigh;
an aeroplane I cannot hear has shark fins
and three black camels sleep in a blue, blue desert.

                          ii
My bowl has cauled my memories. My bowl
has buried me. Hoofprints where Ali's horse
baulked at the glint of cutlasses have thrummed
against my eyelids. Caves where tribal women
stooped to place tin sconces, their tapers lit,
have scaffolded my skin. Limpet pools
have scooped my gums, raising weals and the blue
of morning glory furled around my limbs.

My bowl has smashed my boundaries: harebell
and hawthorn mingling in my thickened waist
of jasmine; catkin and *chenar*, dwarf oak
and hazel hanging over torrents, deltas,
my seasons' arteries... *Lahaf-Doozee!*...
My retina is scarred with shadow-dances
and echoes run like hessian blinds across
my sleep; my ears are niches, prayer-rug arches.

Lahaf-Doozee! My backbone is an alley,
a one-way runnelled alley, cobblestoned
with hawkers' cries, a saddlebag of ribs.
The Quilt Man comes. He squats, he stoops, tears strips
of flattened down, unslings his pole of heartwood
and plucks the string: *dang dang tok tok* and cotton
jumping, jumping, leaps to the twang of thread,
leaping, flares in a cloudy hill of fleece.

My ancestors have plumped their quilts with homespun,
in running-stitch have handed down their stories:
an infant in its hammock, safe in cloud,
who swung between two walls an earthquake spared,
hung swaying to and fro, small and holy.
Lizards have kept their watch on lamplight, citrus-
peel in my mother's hand becoming baskets.
My bowl beneath the tap is scoured with leaves.

iii

The white rooms of the house we glimpsed through pine,
quince and pomegranate are derelict.
Calendars of saints' days still cling to plaster,
drawing-pinned. Velvet weavers, hammam keepers
have rolled their weekdays in the rags, the closing
craft bag of centuries. And worker bees
on hillsides, hiding in ceramic jars,
no longer yield the gold of robbers' honey.

High on a ledge, a white angora goat bleats...
I too will take my bowl and leave these wheatfields
speckled with hollyhocks, campanulas,
the threshing-floors on roofs of sundried clay.
Over twigbridge, past camel-thorn and thistle
bristling with snake, through rock rib and ravine
I will lead my mule to the high ground, kneel
above the eyrie, spread my rug in shade.

Below me, as the sun goes down, marsh pools
will glimmer red. *Sineh Sefid* will be gashed
with gold, will change from rose to blue, from blue
to grey. My bowl will hold the bowl of sky
and as twilight falls I will stand and fling
its spool and watch it land as lake: a ring
where *rood* and river meet in peacock blue
and peacock green and a hundred rills cascade.

And evening's narrow pass will bring me down
to bowl, to sit at lakeside's old reflections:
those granite spurs no longer hard and cold
but furred in the slipstream of a lone oarsman.
And from its lap a scent will rise like Mer
of mother love and waters; scent whose name
I owe to Talat, gold for grandmother:
Maryam, tuberose, for bowl, for daughter.

Ghazal: The Servant

Ma'mad, hurry, water the rose.
Blessed is the English one that grows
          out in the rain.

Water is scarce, blood not so.
Blood is the open drain that flows
          out in the rain.

Bring in the lamp, the olive's flame.
Pity the crippled flame that blows
          out in the rain.

Where are the children? What is the time?
Time is the terror curfew throws
          out in the rain.

Hurry, Ma'mad, home to your child.
Wherever my namesake, Maryam, goes
          out in the rain.

Rubaiyat

for Telajune

Beyond the view of crossroads ringed with breath
her bed appears, the old-rose covers death
has smoothed and stilled; her fingers lie inert,
her nail-file lies beside her in its sheath.

The morning's work over, her final chore
was 'breaking up the sugar' just before
siesta, sitting crosslegged on the carpet,
her slippers lying neatly by the door.

The image of her room behind the pane,
though lost as the winding road shifts its plane,
returns on every straight, like signatures
we trace on glass, forget and find again.

I have inherited her tools: her anvil,
her axe, her old scrolled mat, but not her skill;
and who would choose to chip at sugar cones
when sugar cubes are boxed beside the till?

The scent of lilacs from the road reminds me
of my own garden: a neighbouring tree
grows near the fence. At night its clusters loom
like lantern moons, pearly-white, unearthly.

I don't mind that the lilac's roots aren't mine.
Its boughs are, and its blooms. It curves its spine
towards my soil and litters it with dying
stars: deadheads I gather up like jasmine.

My grandmother would rise and take my arm,
then sifting through the petals in her palm
would place in mine the whitest of them all:
'Salaam, dokhtaré-mahé-man, salaam!'

'Salaam, my daughter-lovely-as-the-moon!'
Would that the world could see me, Telajune,
through your eyes! Or that I could see a world
that takes such care to tend what fades so soon.

from *Interiors*

after Edouard Vuillard

Edouard Vuillard (1868-1940) lived with his mother until her death
when he was 50. Mme Vuillard was a seamstress and her workroom, like
his studio, was part of the home. 'The home and the studio were one,
and the honour of the home and the honour of the studio the same
honour. What resulted? Everything was a rhythm, a rite and a ceremony
from the moment of rising. Everything was a sacred event...'

Charles Péguy, *l'Argent*

The Parlour

Between the cup and lip,
needle and the cloth,
closing of a cupboard door
and the reassertion of a room,

in those pauses of the eye
when the head lifts and time stands still

what gesture slips its epoch
to evoke another continent?
What household conjures household

in the homogeneity of furniture,
rituals that find their choirs
in morning light, evening lamps,
cloths and clothes and screens?

This woman sewing,
man reading at his desk,
in raising eyes towards the wall
do they lose themselves in foliage,

sense themselves receding
to become presences on gravel paths
and in becoming incorporeal
free to be transposed?

Do they see themselves and not themselves
— have any sense how manifold
might be their incarnations —
in the needlepoint of walls and skies
so distant from their own?

For this profile hazed
against shutterfold and sky
has as many claimants
as there are flowers on the wall,
in a vase, on a dress, in the air

and everywhere, like leaves,
recognitions drop their calling-cards
on a mood, a table set for supper,

disperse themselves as freely
as the mille-fleurs from a palette,

settle unobtrusively
as her to her sewing, him to his book,
lowering eyes from vistas
that have brought them to themselves.

The Workroom

It was in the whirring of a treadle,
biting of a thread,
resumption of the treadle

while eyes were closed
and shadows of the scissors
like the noon sun through its zenith
were passing overhead,

that allegiances were fed their rhythms,
loyalties first given shape.

With a lever sprung, a length released,
launched in its wake on a sea of stuffs,
flecks of wool, waves of walnut grain,

given food and drink, we gave
the thanks we never knew in time
we would strive to give, to keep alive
in words, in songs, in paint.

It was in these gestures, the day's devotions,
with a pockmarked thumb, pinheads
jammed in a mouth that held them safe,
that an inheritance was slowly stitched,

a paradigm to give body to
like a second life to curtains,
a lining to a dress. And now
when prayers we never knew were prayers

in the guise of silver bobbins,
machines we never mastered,
are once again at work
in the hands of daughters making light

of the partnering, unpartnering of threads;
when voices caught, then thought lost
in transit while ours in vows
were still keeping faith,

return in transpositions
in a dream like a revelation,
familial as they were in life
to orchestrate our states of grace;

how can we not fail them?
What sacraments can we find but these
poor leavings of a memory
of a home, a time, a place?

Studies for the Workroom

With an arm along a table,
a head against an arm
and the sensation of an eye

from the highest corner of the room
that looks down, sees only

our right side laid
in folds of light
while shadows on its underside
pulsate against an ear,

how childhood in its timelessness
like a fishspine between sun and moon

in this laying out of halves,
this pool of concentricity,
luxuriates!

★

And though the head stays still
while the mind, listing against currents,
logs driftwood on its way,

on frequencies faint
as lilacs in a beige

is such a weightlessness of objects,
scumbling of their outlines
that volition, like a craft

fazed by would-be voyagers
– colours and their offspring,
rhythms and their cargo –

is arrested at the rivermouth
while on the deck the masts,
long antennae of a daydream,

frame a stillness that might pass
for idleness.

★

While journeys made
are left hanging in their harbours,
hanging in farewells,

journeys daydreams sail on
surprise themselves with atolls:
an atoll in an Indian ocean

where birds that have lost their power of flight
because they have no enemies

make scissor-runs across sand and tide –
poignant, being flightless,
more poignant, being safe.

★

Drops of sweat fall on lawn, go grey
and white again under the iron's nose
as steam clears.

It clears on fields
sewn one to another,
braided with a hedge.

On the far side of the hedge
is nothing:
no life except one's own,
the sky's, trees', clouds',

nothing where there ought to be
the promise that was given
when one thought of looking here.

Tacking in an armhole
flashes semaphore and sunray.

★

Through banging in the kitchen,
cousins' voices drifting
out of space, through liquid

slugging into jugs
and the smell of olive oil
– tomato pips like frog-spawn
pooled on small glass plates –

comes the punctuation of a reverie,
a summons arcing over chairs.

A disc of air, bright or warm
to walk towards,

forms when they call one's name.

★

The lever of the Singer
is a long slick thumb.

Like saintliness
stern
on its own small world,

it sets the eye in motion:
level with an upper world,
lower world, whether

an empty eye, threaded eye,
eye that sees no difference
between function and futility,
action and mimicry, riding

gaily on its open slot,
its silver pole, its carousel.

★

Once the wheel is turned,
articulations of the lever
folded under cover for the night

and the need for counting stops
as blankets open up their triangles,
tartan rugs their squares,

those whose closing eyes rely
on an eye that keeps its vigil
empowered in the dark to see
brighter in their stead, know,

relinquishing without resentment
their weight beneath its power,
how darkness can illumine

what day hid, life hid, to eyes
that grow accustomed to its glare.

Studies for the Parlour

As the ear is to the orchestration
of sounds near and far, mingling, overlaid,

an orchestra in which the human voice
is an accent as a bird's is, the ring
of cutlery on glass, trowel on brick,

so too the eye,
seeing wallpaper as fabric,
a baby's cheek as millboard,
a butterfly
large and white above a path
that turns out to be a passerby
receding down a lane,

is, to the hierarchies of vision, blind
but by some law of mimetism
able to convey

not only sounds and tastes and smells
but the workings of memory itself,
short circuiting, choosing what it will

to light on, without a thought
for boundaries, vocabularies
that distinguish the substances
our world and we are made of,
landscape from flesh.

★

Counting beads, apple pips, tiny things
only we are small enough to count on,
colours by their overlaps

stained, fatigued, in sun-leached lengths
reds no longer red;
turning marbles to the light

and marking indentations, the surface
scratch that tells us where we are
and were before is still the same,

we hold tomorrows solid
in the promise of days to come
when pips give way to orchards –
apple-green, plum-blue, gooseberry-red.

Little do we dream though
that larger minds at ease
with magnitude, expansion,

will be as nonplussed as we are
by the small become dimensionless,
the infinite nonsensical,
by particles as fuzzy

as the kitten in the parlour
collapsing like a star
as it turns to catch its tail.

★

Caught between desire
to enter sitting-rooms illicitly,
standing huge among the ornaments,
chairs we dare not sit on in the presence
of the air's thin wraiths,

and the line of least resistance
to rooms we have the run of
among the largenesses of elders
whose bustling is our luxury,
our leave to be ignored in,

we hover on a landing
between the handle and the stairs:

for stowed away with odours, whispers,
mirrors where the souls of those we love
are skyed like chandeliers,

dimensions we know nothing of
– of lives played out before ours began,
games too human or too pitiable
to let us see with the same eyes
the world we saw this morning –

will lure us in with stories,
feed our hunger for the evidence
of crimes we cannot name.

Sauntering back through doorways then,
with an innocence no sooner lost
than reassumed, we take our place
at table, lift our eyes to faces

knowing nothing of our loss
but betraying, for the first time, theirs.

★

These were rooms
we should not have entered
or entering, not taken fright,
fright at their premonitions,

the story with one ending
we would fight against
and in fighting

corrupt the spirit
that is outside the scope of stories
or is the one that has no end.

★

Though morning light and evening light
come, like echoes, friable as gunfire

and faith, in a weakening tug-of-war
between the reality that bombards us
and the will to give a body
to the latency inside us, wilts,

the memory of tables
vibrant with refracted light,
objects now forgotten
on oil cloths or chenilles,

the child cluttering up the doorway,
the hand that eased her in,

the evocation of a lived-in grace
that continues to sustain us
however gracelessly we live,

still connect with a source of love,
that sudden shining open space
to which words, conjoining as they near,
float in.

★

It was those glass-sprigged afternoons
the best part of us was born in.

Now in a fading light – condensation
rising on the panes, snowing us in –
through a veil of milk

it aches, it glows, it passes…

II

Needlework

Within the lamplight's circle,
in the embroidery hoop the flowers,
my name within my lifetime
handed on to no one dies with me.

My knots are neat.
My cottage gardens will be stretched
with the ones my daughters stitch.
My youngest keeps me company.

On an upper landing where my work
is hung, in another century,
some strange and foreign woman
may try to picture me

and fail. Or is it that I fail
to picture her? I cannot think
what she would want with me.
With hollyhocks and bonnets.

The Woman in the Wall

Why they walled her up seems academic.
They have their reasons. She was a woman
with a nursing child. Walled she was
and dying. But even when they surmised

there was nothing of her left but dust and ghost,
at dawn, at dusk, at intervals
the breast recalled, wilful as the awe
that would govern village lives, her milk flowed.

And her child suckled at the wall, drew
the sweetness from the stone and grew
till the cracks knew only wind and weeds
and she was weaned. Centuries ago.

Stone of Patience

'In the old days,' she explained to a grandchild bred in England,
'in the old days in Persia, it was the custom to have a stone,
a special stone you would choose from a rosebed, a goat-patch,
a stone of your own to talk to, tell your troubles to,
a stone we called, as they now call me, a stone of patience.'

No therapists then to field a question with another
but stones from dust where ladies' fingers, cucumbers
curled in sun. Were the ones they used for gherkins
babies that would have grown, like piano tunes had we known
the bass beyond the first few bars? Or miniatures?

Some things I'm content to guess – colour in a crocus-tip,
is it gold or mauve? A girl or a boy... Patience
was so simple then, waiting for the clematis to open,
to purple on a wall, the bud to shoot out stamens,
the jet of milk to leave its rim like honey on the bee's fur.

But patience when the cave is sealed, a boulder
at the door, is riled by the scent of hyacinth
in the blue behind the stone: a willow by the pool
where once she sat to trim a beard with kitchen scissors,
to tilt her hat at smiles, sleep, congratulations.

And a woman faced with a lover grabbing for his shoes
when women friends would have put themselves in hers
no longer knows what's virtuous. Will anger shift
the boulder, buy her freedom and the earth's? Or patience,
like the earth's, be abused? Even nonchalance

can lead to courage, conception: a voice that says
'Oh come on darling, it'll be alright, do let's.'
How many children were born from words such as these?
I know my own were, now learning to repeat them, to outgrow
a mother's awe of consequence her body bears.

CHILD: NEW AND SELECTED POEMS

So now that midsummer, changing shape, has brought in
another season, the grape becoming raisin, hinting
in a nip at the sweetness of a clutch, one fast upon another;
now that the breeze is raising sighs from sheets
as she tries to learn again, this time for herself,

to fling caution to the winds like colour in a woman's skirt
or to borrow patience from the stones in her own backyard
where fruit still hangs on someone else's branch... don't ask her
'whose?' as if it mattered. Say 'they won't mind'
as you reach for a leaf, for the branch, and pull it down.

Overblown Roses

She held one up, twirling it in her hand
as if to show me how the world began
and ended in perfection. I was stunned.
How could she make a rose so woebegone,
couldn't silk stand stiff? And how could a child,
otherwise convinced of her mother's taste,
know what to think? *It's overblown*, she smiled,
I love roses when they're past their best.

'Overblown roses', the words rang in my head,
making sense as I suddenly saw afresh
the rose now, the rose ahead: where a petal
clings to a last breath; where my mother's flesh
and mine, going the same way, may still
be seen as beautiful, if these words are said.

from *Plant Care*

Cacti need little water; miniatures
barely a drop. A teaspoon each, she said,
or fill the tray. It waits on the melodeon
crammed with tiny pots that are all in flower
– pinwheel yellows, tousled fists of red –
so light, so dry, with a touch they topple over.

Lack of oestrogen makes women shrink.
While tall, thin, white women like Beverlie
are prone to osteoporosis, small women
like myself shrink even smaller. Our line
of nonagenarians cobwebs our family tree
where small old women hang like drops of dew.

    Feed me stew and stock of marrow,
    beetroot sliced and sweet to swallow.
    Veil me white in flowery lawn,
    meadow eyebright, moth mullein.

All bones and bones from yard to bed,
all knuckled knees and lolling head,
and when I move draw back the veil,
let death fly out and sing its tale:

Left fist, right fist,
which is the fist I hide it in?
Sweet and joke and tethering-rope,
your navel-chord and na-ame.

Left fist, right fist,
fool's gold, wishbone,
who's to know where the devil to dig,
the ground all looks the sa-ame.

★

My mother's postcard shows a carpet stall
where men in long white tunics, short blue waistcoats
are staring at a *farangi* in a trilby
and a Philip Marlowe trenchcoat. Above them
a plaque reads: FARSH FOROOSHI AHMADIAN.
Pleasant and peaceful flight, arrived safely.
Happy I came. Haven't been round the town yet –
a town whose peeling skins of war await her,
as Ahmadian himself might once have stood,
deferential, in his fraying cuffs
beside the beaded curtain:

                              Befarmayid.
Gholam, bring tea, a *ghalian*... Welcome.
May your shadow at my door ever lengthen.
Here is a sanctum, serpentine and cushion-
cool where guinea-fowl and golden hind
wind on the banks of silk between us, leagues
of flowing patterns please us, heavens themselves
descend to earth where stars may catch our heels.
Sugar? May Allah bring what Allah wills.
I tell no tales. May God protect your children.

In an older dream I had, the wash-basin
was in a room but also under trees
whose lower branches hung along the soap-ledge
so when I ran the water it took colour
from the petals: pink and gold. And the water
fanned carnelian pink and saffron gold
till pink and gold ran pale and spectre-thin
and petals, drained, now lay like cabbage whites
and nothing I could do, no urging, willing,
could make the water colour. Later, waking,
I thought how even in my dreams I mutter
magic runs in holes they know nothing of in England.

★

I wish to make tall statements,
to say that life is... dot dot dot,
blue polka-dot, forget-me-not... I cannot. All
I can say is, that as a child...

and the voices are lost... lost...
and the word that is said
                    said twice, said twice
since we, the infant opening eyes
at the left breast, right breast,
heard once, then twice, the gobbledy-gook
of her twin-drum sighs: *Bokhor! Bokhor!*
and drank and drank as we rose and sank
on the housecoat, houseboat, as the clock ticked
    and the groundswell shrank to a plea...
then we were children running past
on the lawn (oh, the lawn where they sat at cards!)
who heard on the left and heard on the right
– the engine near, the ocean far –
the one, the two, the nation cry:
Go slow! Go slow! *Yavosh! Yavosh!*
and laughed and wheeled and ran on fast.

Why, dust on my head, they'll break their necks!
My measle-child! My beetle-black!
Elahi, sister! Brother, run!
Oh, hurry and catch-as-catch-can!

Nahzi, nahzi, gol-é-piyahzi!
There, my love, my flowering bulb,
Allah be praised, she's only grazed,
fetch me a drop, a watering-can.

★

I meet my sister in the garden; her barrow is alive with plants:
　　shrub and herb and creeper.

I know what you have carried all these years, my sister cries:
　　like the running of the loam across my nails.

If the plant is left unstaked, shoots must find their own mouths:
　　prayers turn inward on themselves.

As she has been my water, so I shall be her cane:
　　on the seventh day, on the fortieth day, in one year's time,
　　on known and unknown anniversaries of death.

But who is the God who wields the sword, who blesses those that
take our children and throw them against the stones:
　　who is the man that said, *If I had only two loaves of bread,*
　　I would barter one for hyacinths to nourish my soul?

Now we are the shortest line between two points:
　　ancient brackets on either side of earth's long shelf.

God's big book is all that stands between us:
　　where mother would have stood, her arms around our shoulders,
　　the scent of death's head honey in her hair.

Let us lean against her shrine, light our cigarettes:
　　smoke is rising through the dust, curling like a vine above
　　our heads.

We have heard the falling bombs, sat away from breaking glass:
　　here, on the sofa, where I held you in my arms, your voice
　　at my feet calling through the clay.

Let us take our turn together:
　　let us die as we have lived.

And neither live to live alone:
　　fire without water, earth without air.

★

Now we are the album-bearers,
wondering who and where
is the one who left the fresh black square,
whose two-year-olds, three-year-olds,
come back to us, exactly as they were,
only in dreams. They pose in sharp white frills
on breakwaters, scoop eddies into sky blue buckets
at our heels, now we are the breast milk dreamers
who wake with words unformed... where is the tongue,
the air's wet mouth, dear Lord, where is
the mouth, the clamp to take me in?

It is a dispossession, a market we are led to
not knowing what to barter, bid for, value more
than blood's red witch or the snowqueen's wealth...
though centre-frame, from mouths of distant tents,
like triumvirs in the desert, crones beckon:

     Have you come for oral history,
     a final heaping of your plate?

     Come to sample wisdom's wine?
     Or burn and pray for rain?

     Are these your fists whose ink runs dry
     when it comes to stake your claim?

     No. Let go my elbow.
     I, too, have stood my ground

     dreading to become
     the dreaded figure I became.

There is a dip in every dune where the urn
takes shape, sand begins to caul protecting
foetal forms and the gorse quickens...

I hear no footfall, see no change.

River Sonnet

Welling up in her fingers, water runnelled
seaward through stones. She wasn't watching water.
Or thinking of tomorrow – how time funnelled,
flows. Water was doing her thinking for her.
Draining down her thoughts till they ran as lightly
as leaves across a playground, rose to torment
branches that had borne them, betrayed them, nightly
blurred distinctions, daily held to their bent
and finally torn loose. She heard the river
babble, level, contradictions resolve
in a rush, out of her hands, felt quarrels fly
in droves. *Who-o-o* the river sang, *who-so-ever*
clouds rang round the sky, sky thinking itself
in river, river thinking itself in sky.

Come Close

'Come close', the flower says and we come close,
close enough to lift, cup and smell the rose,
breathe in a perfume deep enough to find
language for it but, words having grown unkind,

think back instead to a time before we knew
what we know now. When every word was true
and roses smelt divine. What went wrong?
Long before the breath of a cradle song.

Some lives fall, some flower. And some are granted
birthrights – a verandah, a sunken quadrant
of old rose trees, a fountain dry as ground
but still a fountain, in sense if not in sound.

Like a rose she slept in the morning sun.
Each vein a small blue river, each eyelash shone.

Blue Moon

Sitting on a windowsill, swinging
her heels against the wall as the gymslips
circled round and Elvis sang Blue Moon,

she never thought one day to see her daughter,
barelegged, sitting crosslegged on saddlebags
that served as sofas, pulling on an ankle

as she nodded sagely, smiling, not denying –
you'll never catch me dancing to the same old tunes;
while her brother, strewed along a futon,

grappled with his Sinclair, setting up
a programme we'd asked him to. Tomorrow
he would teach us how to use it but for now

he lay intent, pale, withdrawn, peripheral
in its cold white glare as we went up to our rooms:
rooms we once exchanged, like trust, or guilt,

each knowing hers would serve the other better
while the other's, at least for now, would do.
The house is going on the market soon.

My son needs higher ceilings; and my daughter
sky for her own blue moon. You can't blame her.
No woman wants to dance in her Mum's old room.

Boy in a Photograph

The wind is up and as we
wind down it grows harder, colder, harsher.
He is the boy,

arms around his knees
like a shepherd in a loincloth
dappled under trees,

who gazed out to the hills
where life somewhere else raced faster.
His watchface even now

is scudding on his wrist,
tracking like a ninja-cloud
following its master. (The wind

was up but has changed its mind,
only leaves in close-up
are blowing harder...)

What was it he was gazing at
across those hills, eyes trained
on a flare, ears keened to a call

of horizons? We have captured him
and blown him up, in shade, in youth,
while his unseen flock

– what flock, what fleece? –
grows larger, smaller, larger.

The Piano

You have found your digital metronome.
Where, you didn't say. I have never said,
or always said in so many words, how a piano
is nothing to the weight I bear. Your throat
so soft, feet bare, where you played the violin
in pyjamas, and the black and white cat whose instinct
for camouflage would draw him to the stool
when we weren't there – you didn't find it there.

Downstairs. On the ground floor of our lives.
Nor, in a flat whose floors walk into trees,
was it anywhere near the old metronome,
broken, mechanical, you'd repositioned;
flung aside with your oval clock I rescued,
reassembled, dismissed the corner sliver
of glass no one'll notice. The piano tuner
didn't steal it then. – Just as well.

A body is a thing of dread. A thing
of guilt. Desire and dream. Something
to purge with percussion. How rare it is
to merge with, to have your own organs sing
through another's. See, it has taken blindness
from your touch, the grime you took from newsprint,
down escalator rails. Milk will revive
its ivory. It must be cared for in silence.

And even a piano must have water.
Be tempered to the precise pitch of health.
How it hurts you. Hurts where you have already
hurt yourself. It is in step. I will take
the shawl it has worn so long only washing,
ruining, will remove its folds and dents.
I don't want to remove them. Such a worn-in
fit is rare. I am cold. I'm cold, Tom, play.

from *The Inwardness of Elephants*

Elephant Man

Films about the British Empire
are invariably monochrome – sepia – the colour
of tea and biscuits my son says and we laugh

in one of my fields of tenderness.
He himself is a field. Taller than
the tallest grasses, higher than the highest

mast in a bay. He faces the horizon,
hides his eyes by facing the other way.
He has tried travel. The song of whales.

He himself is the music he cannot play.
I am the wrong note he says. I change
my tune but I'm no piper, and my range

smaller than my strength belies and my breath
smokier every day. Of all the songs earth's
creatures sing, I aspire to the elephant's rumble

too bass for man to hear. Because it covers
distance, because it moves the herd. Mothers
are always wrong. Whatever the song,

whatever the note of anger, love, despair.
And their song travels deep inside them,
down to their boots, down to the roots they tear.

My son stares out of his eyes as if to torch
his brain. He covers his head in a towel
for the world is covered with jawbones, burial

grounds the thaw reveals, I look like
Elephant Man he says. He eats his meal.
Potatoes mostly. Shovels them through the crack.

White Gold

Back from India, my daughter gives me
a carved filigree elephant, a baby
inside it tooled from the same grey flesh.

Is it ivory? I ask, as if chinoiseries,
chessmen, dominoes, combs, piano keys,
daggers, rifle butts, hunting horns,

inlaid pulpits and mosque doors, Zeus
at Olympia, Athena in the Parthenon,
Tutankhamun's chair, Solomon's throne,

weren't enough white gold plundered,
not to mention hair and tails turned
into fly whisks, ears into tables,

feet into umbrella stands and even
eyelashes sold to guarantee fertility
and the desired number of children.

No, she says. And my cow proliferates.
On boxes, bedspreads, mugs, cushions,
in jasper, wood, brass, ceramic processions.

My favourite elephants are on a black
glasses case: two calves embroidered
in shades of pink, one rose on powder,

the other reversed. I attract them the way
I do children: a whole orphanage of elephants
on presents, cards, surrounds me on my birthday

and from Oregon come cuttings – Chendra
has anaemia, Pet eye surgery, and in Kenya,
when there is no ivory, there are no orphans.

Mahout

We trust each our own elephant
till our own elephant kills us.
The attendants holding the silk umbrellas,

the one who plies the fan
of peacock feathers, the man
with the flyswatter of yaktails.

You cannot cheat on the amount of oil
poured in the lamps for an elephant
will always honour the pace of the ritual.

Nor is the elephant's love less manifest.
He will insert his trunk, like a hand,
inside your garments and caress your breast.

He will follow, with his mate,
the undulations in B minor of *Iphigenia in Tauris*
or, on solo bassoon, *Oh, my Tender Musette.*

And the cow will stroke him with her long
and flexible member before bringing
it back upon herself, pressing its finger

first in her mouth, then in his ear.
While over their transports, whistling fire,
the harmony of two human voices

falls like summer rain.
Meat that walks like a mountain
among giant flowers, huge nettles and lobelia.

Child, don't be afraid.
The mandala of nine precious stones
is never absent from his forehead.

Soapstone Creek

The creek sings all night long and all night long
we listen in our sleep, waking from dreams
we recognise as our own undersong
to grief, a gabble of diverted streams

under the paths our lives took, our children's lives
we listened to so avidly but missed
the earliest signs where the ground first gives,
tracks to the water in our own tracks twist,

thinking how blessed we were, wise our choices,
skirting the treacherous silt. Yet all the while
those streams, under the cover of animal voices,
were making a mockery of free will.

Nothing's as constant as the creek. The silence
of the forest depends on it. Our deeds,
misdeeds, omissions too, make no more sense
than rattle-cries, flung where the kingfisher breeds.

Under the alders' canopy that steals
their share of sunlight, understory trees,
spread their leaves as they may, can only feel
sun sideways. And some grow accordingly.

Soapstone Retreat

Late summer sun is falling through the forest.
As if the forest knew it would soon turn yellow,
it shifts a little, stars in the creek below
signalling to the sunlight on its crest.

In the centre it is still. Still late August.
On the periphery, branches, leaves, follow
the scent of autumn. Like a woodfire slow
to get going after the stove's long rest,

the forest stirs with ambivalent longings
for movement, stillness, as if its life were elsewhere
but its heart were here. And as cold nights near,

these last sweet sips at the cusp of the year
hang suspended in the balance as the flask swings,
hummingbird feeds and the sun sinks, stair by stair.

The Robin and the Eggcup

A robin flew into my room today,
into the sun of it, the wood, the plants.

A robin flew into my sleep today,
once for mischief, twice for very good luck.

A robin flew into my soul today,
queried it, rose and flumped against its glass.

So I opened it and the cold came in,
I levered it wide and the bird flew out.

Not for the first time. I let it out too,
my son said, out of the kitchen window.

No! When? Earlier, when you were asleep.
It broke an eggcup. Eggcup! What eggcup?

Not one of those nice blue and white eggcups.
Yes, he said joyfully, I swept it up.

Motherhood

Suppose I emptied my flat of everything,
everything but my books? The elephants
would have to go. They'd be the first to go
– being the youngest – and the last, the plants
perhaps, relics of early motherhood.
I'd keep the piano, all my files and photos.

I'd keep my grandmother's chest to keep my photos
in, in and not on top of, everything
swept absolutely clear of motherhood.
Nothing shall move: no herd of elephants
proceed down my mantelpiece, spider plants
produce babies, carpets moths, moths shall go

into the ether where all bad spells go.
I'm sick of the good. Of drooling over photos
that lie, lie, lie, breaking my back over plants
for whom – *Oh! for whom?* Not everything
I thought green greened. Not even elephants
consoled me for the bane of motherhood.

Therefore motherhood must go. Motherhood
must go as quietly as prisoners go
and all her things go with her, elephants
troop behind her, tapestries drown her, photos –
OK photos can stay but everything
dust-collecting goes the way of the plants.

Everything shall live in name only. Plants
now extinct shall be extolled, motherhood
shall be blessed but not mothers, everything
everywhere being their fault though they go
to the dock protesting, producing photos
of happy toddlers, citing elephants,

rashly, as preceptors since elephants,
however vicious they may be to plants
or photographers with blinding flash photos,
are the very model of motherhood.
Such are the myths of nature. They shall go.
There shall be room, time, space, for everything:

room in the wild for elephants and plants,
time to go rummaging a chest for photos,
space for everything cleared of motherhood.

Apology

Humming your Nocturne on the Circle Line,
unlike the piano, running out of breath

I've been writing you out of my life
my loves (one out, one in).

I've pushed you out of the way to see
what the gaps in my life might look like,

how large they are,
how quickly I could write them in;

and not (at least till I've lost you both)
rewriting you only means

that the spaces I'm not writing in are where
I live.

Sundays

for Tom

i

Together, we have made sour cherry rice,
rolled minced lamb into meatballs and listened
to the radio while eating, him to stall
hallucinations and me to respect his silence,

the time he takes to eat. We've strolled slowly
in the park together, our favourite park,
lapsing into pauses with the falling light –
tennis in the distance – as we slowly climbed

the hill. I've left my shoes at the door, him
reminding me, to scrub off the dogshit later
and now he's at the piano in the nowhere hour
before TV. These are the things that make him

well – company, old and easy, recipes
old but new to him. His playing brings
the night in. Turns the streetlamps on, makes
the kitchen clock tick. Softly a chord falls

and out of the ground grow snowdrops, fat
and waxy, with green hearts stamped upside down
on aprons, poking their heads through railings.
Between his fingers things grow, little demons,

fountains, crocuses. Spring is announced and enters,
one long green glove unfingering the other,
icicles melt and rivers run, bluetits
hop and trill. Everything talks to everything.

ii

How it poured with rain today. My gutter,
blocked and inaccessible to anyone bar
the man with the longest ladder in London,
waterfalled down the window alarmingly.

No, the waterfall is here, under his fingers,
steady wrists, the years of training paying off
in instinctual music; and the fat raindrops, spraying
up like diamanté; and the tailing off

of rain, all the languages of rain, rivers,
gutters, waterfalls, the treble runs
of rain and the bass's percussive beat;
all the liquidity of youth, youth gone

to rack and ruin. How little he ate today
and how much there was to eat – stuffed pepper,
salmon, apple and blackberry tart, coffee.
He can't even swallow his own saliva,

holding it in his mouth minutes at a time,
without hearing them, the voices, seeing
babies streaming towards his mouth, limbs
trigger words command him: that, there, take, eat.

iii

He ate all of it. All of the rice
and all of the *khoreshté bademjan*
– the aubergine dish – I carefully filled
his plate with, not overfilled. He liked it.

He was always sweet about my cooking.
We ate while watching *West Side Story*.
How easy it was to sorrow for Maria
and Tony. Easy to cry and grieve.

Now he's at the piano, today
so tentative but gaining in assurance,
like someone 'learning to live with disability'.
Is he? Or is that someone me?

all of us, all of us who love him.
Joey rings. He's free tomorrow,
Tom's saying – he hasn't decided yet
whether to stay with me a while,

I hope he will. And suddenly
there's sunshine, brightness and a bounce
and his fingers are dancing. Voices
might bedevil him but voices also

save him – Moss's, Joey's, Sara's –
or let him down without meaning to,
without knowing, after they've finished
a call, the music stops again

as suddenly as it started. But now
he's into it – and what's that tune?
coming and going. Tom, what's that tune?
'All the Things You Are' he tells me.

Tintinnabuli

How sad he was, Arvo Pärt,
not to have thanked his teacher
for the parting thought she gave him:

that the biggest mystery in music
is something about – he couldn't
remember her exact words –

something about how to enter
a single sound, just as his janitor,
when asked how should a composer

compose, replied: he has to love
each sound, each sound – so that
every blade of grass would be,

Pärt adds, as important as the flower
(and the bent man on the bent road
picking raspberries, the soprano

holding a green pencil to mark
on her score where to breathe)
and the soul yearn to sing it endlessly.

This one note, or a silent beat, or a moment of silence,
comforts me. I build with primitive materials –
with the triad, with one specific tonality.

The three notes of a triad are like bells
and that is why I call it tintinnabulation.
Tintinnabuli – itself the sound of grass,

blades moving like bells, harebells say,
though there are no flowers but stems alone
and a breath of wind to give the grass direction.

Ghazal: The Children

The children are not ours
but the child they might have been
    is in their eyes.
The children live in camps
but the freedom they have seen
    is in their eyes.

The children wear boleros,
beads and kaftans, tribal
    paint and feathers,
sandals in the snow and *hejab*
as white as snow whose sheen
  is in their eyes.

The children stand with younger
children on their hips,
    in their arms.
Like animals at grass,
stopping in a day's routine
    is in their eyes.

The children hold belongings –
pens and notebooks, blankets,
    shoes and saucepans;
their fingers tell us stories
and what these stories mean
    is in their eyes.

The children are not ours
but you, Salgado, have brought them
    this close, this far.
I stand within a hand's-breadth
and the world that lies between
    is in their eyes.

III

from *Entries on Light*

Sunday. I woke
　　from a raucous night of
seagulls, shafts of sun
　　in old bazaars where motes spun

on an abacus for angels.
　　Do you long
to go back to that childhood
　　the angels asked

in a grown-up body?
　　the everlasting blue enquired
as I woke
　　to skies washed clean of dust

and churchbells.
　　From the acorn of the blind
such seas came
　　such tall grave oaks!

Acorn-greys
　　of the sea, its pennant rocks
where cormorant wings
　　are omens... *Do you long*

to go back to that childhood
　　the waters asked
in a grown-up body?
　　the everlasting shore enquired

with a cockerel
　　to wake me in the morning
a dog to guard us
　　through the night, one window

pink with sunset, one blue
　　with dusk? I could go on and on.
But I am moving into the morning.
　　I am making do with light.

Today's grey light
    is of
light withheld but
    softly
shyly like a sheltered
    girl's.

It's a
    light in gentle
motion
    like a young girl
sitting
    splaying her skirts

her listening smiles
    around her.
When
    barefoot
she disappears
    momentarily to another

sky
    gleams like glassware
we can hear not see
    we
contract but air
    expands

into a memory
    she has thrown
behind her.
    And in the memory is
light
    and lightness.

Scales are evenly
    weighed, inside
outside. Light is
    evenly poised
– blur to the gold
    glare to the blue –
it's twilight.
    In two minds.

Who can read by
    a lamp, focus
land's outline?
    But blue soon
sinks and gold
    rises. Who
can stay the balance
    if light can't?

The heavier, fuller, breast
    and body grow, the higher
flies the thought, the more
    rarefied its air.

It is the law of action:
    the stronger a gesture, the lighter
its recovery. On a black sea
    how far the spirit sails!

I hear myself in the loudness
   of overbearing waves, you
in the soft retreat, if-and-but
   of withdrawing sighs, the tug
that gets me nowhere.
   It'll never end. Sound
of the sea — still Sappho's sea —
   the yes-and-no of lovers.

Inland, I dreamt of hearing
   waves again but here
sea in my ears, watching reds
   of life-jackets, blues
of a hull and sails, recapture
   in the yes-and-no of my own blood
only the to-and-fro of our endless
   drift — my bed a beach, you said.

Everything I ever said about you
   was true; but trueness
in that tone and at that pitch
   never helps. How could we help
having loved elsewhere too much
   and I don't mean other lovers
but homelands, other cultures
   pulling oceans in their wake?

Speak to me as shadows do
    where light comes through
perforations of snow-white lace

attenuating on a surface
    eyelets into ovals
softening prisms into flakes.

Speak to me as echoes do
    attenuating, softening
the thing first harshly said.

It's all very well
    for me you think and I
for trees and sky and wind;
    blind to the grief
beyond our walls, who can tell
    what shadow falls, or leaf?

Light's taking a bath tonight
    in the sea's enamelled
blue-rimmed bath, lying along
    its length. Hair submerged
thighs and belly in mile-long
    strips showing through white
between limbs and fingers
    bluer depths.

Light's closing her eyes
    not once but twice – once
face up, once facing down
    from her ceiling mirror.
In rising steam, the longest
    bath earth's ever seen, closing
her lids on sea and sky till only
    mist and vapour stir.

    With finest needles
        finest beads
    lawn and dew are making
        a tapestry of water...

Dawn paves its own way
    if what we mean by dawn
is sunrise. The sky's already
    light by the time the sun
comes up, rising on its own
    prediction of the day.
This is how art is made.
    And memory. And love.

First, the halo overhead.
    Next, the body. Last
the roots like the final
    rays of the sun spiralling
as earth pulls free of them
    and they of earth. Then
illumination's width and frame.
    This is how love is made

rising into a desire
    for love, however grey
the outlook, late the hour
    hard for faith and fear
to pave the way. Love
    full-face. Preordained
as sunrise, chasing after
    the ghost of its own grace.

Everywhere you see her, who could have been
    Monet's woman with a parasol
who's no woman at all but an excuse for wind –
    passage of light and shade we know
wind by – just as his pond was no pond
    but a globe at his feet turning to show
how the liquid, dry, go topsy-turvy, how far
    sky goes down in water. Like iris, agapanthus
waterplants from margins where, tethered
    by their cloudy roots, clouds grow underwater
and on lily-pads, two by two, mayflies hover
    waiting for departure, she comes at a slant
to crosswinds, currents, against shoals of sunlight
    set adrift, loans you her reflection.
I saw her the other day I don't know where
    at a tangent to some evening, to a sadness
she never shares. She wavers, like recognition.
    Something of yours goes through her, something
of hers escapes. To hillbrows, meadows
    where green jumps into her skirt, hatbrim shadows
blind her. To coast, wind at her heels, on diagonals
    as the minute hand on the hour, the hour
on the wheel of sunshades. Everywhere you see her.
    On beaches, bramble paths, terraces of Edwardian
hotels. In antique shops, running her thumb along
    napworn velvet. A nail buffer. An owl brooch
with two black eyes of onyx. Eyes she fingers.
    But usually on a slope. Coming your way.

Don't draw back
   his lilac said.
Don't pin me down
   his blue and grey.
Whose tears are pricking
   eyelids? asked his pink
on snow. Mine, black answered
   mine that light can't shed.

Light comes between us and our grief:
   flushes it out with gold.
And when skies are overcast, still
   we collude with clouds, building
grey to a spur for light that will
   drive us to stand at a distance
from ourselves, small at the barricades
   clouds burst to let grief go.
Light leaves us bereft in one sense
   only to flood us with sensation
bleeding out grief in a bright dissolve.
   There's something I can't hold
in the presence of light, great light, or feel
   as a river might feel for its stones.

One sky is a canvas for jets and
    vapour trails, one
Venetian. One a dawn that may spoil
    or bloom, the other
a perfection. On towerblocks or grand
    canals, roundabouts or
basins. Removal trucks, motorbikes
    icecream vans are gilded
in the one, in the other, silence is golden.
    On a moat in Dresden
there are swans, colonnades in water.
    In the Piazetta everyone
is dressed in white, everything is
    lined with copper.

Some will look for immanence
    in a shadow on the wall sinking
through water, or focus where the shadow ends
    on a bricked diagonal of gold
and remember how sun warms brick and linen
    in offices and houses
how glory that was general
    is particular to them.
One is the glory of the yet-to-be, one
    of a past that reminds us
how we've seen it in our own lives exactly
    as it used to be but were
blinded by those lives, distracted from our own
    perfections.

Black fruit is sweet, white is sweeter.
   Sweeter than any white grape, white fig
is white mulberry, too sweet to eat
   without water.

And water, catching casts of berry
   is bluer in its blue-washed pool
than any sky in living memory, boasting
   hot summers in England.

If England is small
   this corner of heaven
is smaller. Barely two bow-lengths
   but morning as long

as the Garden on the Day of Rising
   and evening the length
of a life so little wasted, little room
   has been left for regret.

Instead there is shade and silence.
   One as deep as the other.
Yet for all their depth, buoyant
   as a salt sea, more buoyant for the scent

of jasmine from four corners; only
   tuberose clutches more at the heart
when the heart's at home but home's
   where the heart grows greyer.

So if I were to tell you in future
   how sweet were the berries
left lying in a bowl
   dried and greyed and inedible

once sweet enough to bring tears
   to your eyes, I swear to God
not a word would ring true, for even truth
   lies in the face of the incomparable.

And had we ever lived
   in my country
you might have asked
   had I returned

were backstreets cool
   in siesta heat
did hawkers call
   the mulberry thrive

on neglect?
   Who can I ask
of mulberry and mint
   courtyard shade

so alive with presence
   when no one's around
but a burning sun
   and grapes, walled-in?

Who can I ask
   to ensure a return
have me to stay, receive
   my gifts?

I loved you so much
   I couldn't bear the thought
of cold water on you
   dripping from your chin, hands

running down your elbow
   as you lifted your face to the sound
of footsteps. Smiled at me
   through water. Even

when the season turned
   and no one walked out of shade
to burn in sun
   you'd run the cold –

how cold your hands were.
   Nowhere, as the season turns
and I walk from shade
   or the smell of shade on a sunless

street, in and out of the shade
   of trees to find
no difference, will someone again
   bowing a silvery

head to a tap, move me
   to the kind of love that registers
on skin's temperature
   every shade of difference.

This book is a seagull whose wings
    you hold, reading journeys between
its feathers. It flutters, dazzles.
    Sings cleanly in shade. Sharpens
your ears to journeys life's taken
    that scraping of a mudguard, tinkling
of stays. Its spine has halved the sun.
    Sun fired it with a nimbus.
A wheelchair passes, crunching on shingle.
    This book, set off by wind, makes you
long for the world, to take lungfuls
    of pleasure, save scraps on quick raids.
So that sated, you turn, blot out the world
    enter another, settle for words.

          : that sky and light and colour
              cloud, clearings

          should raise me, strip me down
              to the bare bones

          of vocabulary – rise fall sea sky
              a tree and not a sycamore

          flower and not a bluebell
              till the agony of daily life

          falls away, like ground from a tilting
              plane, drops far below me.

An Iranian professor I know asked me
    the first time we met, as he'd asked so many
students: *Saheb-del* – how would you say in English
    saheb-del, can you translate it? And each time
he pronounced the words his fingers tolled the air
    like a bell, a benediction. Years have passed.

Saheb means master, owner, companion; *del*
    means heart. Heart's companion, keeper?
Heart's host? And in those years I've asked
    friends who in turn have asked friends
who know Urdu, Farsi, and no one has come up with
    the English for *Saheb-del*. Is it a name

for the very thing that won't translate? And why
    don't I remember having heard it said?
They say it of people who are hospitable, 'godly'
    I'd say it of the professor himself. Trust him
to keep asking, us to keep failing, and if we can't recall
    its tone, tenor, with what word shall we keep faith?

All yellow has gone from the day.
    I'm left with the blues and greys.

Pool of light on the desk.
    Strangely content. Perhaps

night is more my element.
    How white white flowers seem

skin showered, oiled, and the day
    but a night away. The days ahead…

It's the eye of longing
    that I tire of
the eye of fantasy
    lost in the grey horizons.

Having neither the heart
    nor talent for
invention, why should I
    – no child of mist –

be party to this cold
    imagination, its cloak
and hood, smuggled goods
    its faery in the dingle?

Where are my sunlight's
    givens? Near the sun
and far from folk
    an albino child, skin clean

as silver, hair white as
    snow, under the Simorgh's
eye as she flies
    over the Alborz Mountains

years later will hear her cry:
    … behold my might,
For I have cherished thee beneath my plumes
And brought thee up among my little ones

before she ferries him home
    gives him a feather to light
as a signal
    in times of trouble.

But this is my borrowed plumage
    language, more strange to me
than this foster-tongue, this English
    fairy godmother.

It is said
      God created a peacock of light
and placed him
      in front of a mirror.
In the presence
      of God, being so ashamed at his own
beauty, his own
      unutterable perfection, the peacock

broke out in a sweat.
      From the sweat of his nose, God created
the Angels.
      From the sweat of his face, the Throne, Footstool
Tablet of Forms, the Pen
      the heavens and what is in them.
From breast and back
      the Visited House, prophets, holy sites, etc.

From the sweat of his two feet
      God created, from east to west, the earth.
The sea is
      glistening peacock sweat.
Tarmac too.
      From sweat of the peacock's feet of pearl
comes my window view.
      Perhaps I am formed from a trembling

drop on his ankle.
      Cypress, sunflower, bicycle wheels
grass dried in heat
      to the colour of wheat, all, all are
peacock water, peacock dew
      shame and beauty, salt and light
God's peacock
      in his consciousness, walks over.

Why does the aspen tremble
    without a trace of wind?
Under its spire, close
    your eyes, listen.
Listen to Khadijah. Her
    big heart beating.
He is bringing a new wife
    home today. Half her age.
Twice her beauty. Aisha, Aisha.
    Listen to the leaves.
What the Bosnian Moslem women say.
    The story they weave.

Khadijah is not jealous.
    Under the awning she
stands, arms folded.
    Arms she will open wide.
Large, generous Khadijah
    ample-limbed...
But when a horse
    pricks up its ears, backs
two paces, whinnies, a current
    faint as the morning star
runs through her, air around her
    ripples, stills.

Like an arrow loosed from
    a quiver, that impulse
shot from her heart
    is caught in the arms
of aspen, sends a shiver
    through every leaf.
And thereafter, though there are
    no aspens in Arabia
though there is
    no wind, this is why
the aspen trembles
    over the bed's thin stream.

And suppose I left behind
   a portrait inadvertently
like a showercap on a peg
   of this seaview that is hers
and insinuated between its clouds
   strange glimpses of myself
that would alter her view
   not only of me but of the sky
her mornings open out on or
   worse, something of herself

either way some hurt would unfold
   open out its own cloud, like smoke
would streak her air. Her air of…
   Seeing ourselves beautiful
also hurts. No longer what we are
   what we were we love but cannot claim.
Looking up, each time we do
   is a silver seachange pencilling
light, shading, erasing
   each time, each time a change.

And where is the singular moment
   unwritten, that's free of pain?
As if by magic, silver lines
   of the horizon have disappeared.
A black ship rides on grey.
   Between everything is a distance
by which we know ourselves, ever
   smarting in the gaps, between
clouds, ships, a child and his unseen
   parents walking on ahead.

Finally, in a cove
   that cups thin fog
like a hand its thirst
   this indivisibility of
sea and sky like a grey
   pearl between two claws

makes sense: as if a bay
   waisting a horizon, woman
legs twined around a man
   were what were needed
to make the horizontal
   more beautiful, more felt;

to interpose
   between eye and sense
a possibility in containment
   of the infinite becoming part
of what the eye can never see
   but the sense can comprehend.

IV

Vine Leaves

Even the vine leaves shot with sun
have shadow leaves
pressed close on them.

Even the vine is hanging
ones that seem like twos:
a top leaf
on a shadow leaf, its corner slipped,
like invoices in duplicate.

If I stood to look from the other side
with the light behind me,
would I still not see
how the top leaf shot with sun
might be the one that fails to fit
its duplicate

instead of
– standing where I do – seeing
how it is the shadow leaf that fails to fit
and failing

makes the one leaf seem like two
and being two, more beautiful?

The Love Barn

Remember the swallows – or were they
swifts? – in the love barn where the wooden
rail we peered over might have been
the height waves tip out of over
rocky pools or the bar of a certain
Sicilian café scattering waiters
like birds or the fence of a driveway
where lupins grow tall as you were
in the barnlight where we stood, leaning
over a railing, smelling the hay.

Ghazal

after Hafez

However large earth's garden, mine's enough.
One rose and the shade of a vine's enough.

I don't want more wealth, I don't need more dross.
The grape has its bloom and it shines enough.

Why ask for the moon? The moon's in your cup,
a beggar, a tramp, for whom wine's enough.

Look at the stream as it winds out of sight.
One glance, one glimpse of a chine's enough.

Like the sun in bazaars, streaming in shafts,
any slant on the grand design's enough.

When you're here, my love, what more could I want?
Just mentioning love in a line's enough.

Heaven can wait. To have found, heaven knows,
a bed and a roof so divine's enough.

I've no grounds for complaint. As Hafez says,
isn't a ghazal that he signs enough?

Ghazal: To Hold Me

I want to be held. I want somebody near
                        to hold me
when the axe falls, time is called, strangers appear
                        to hold me.

I want all that has been denied me. And more.
Much more than God in some lonely stratosphere
                        to hold me.

I want hand and eye, sweet roving things, and land
for grazing, praising, and the last pioneer
                        to hold me.

I want my ship to come in, crossing the bar,
before my back's so bowed even children fear
                        to hold me.

I want to die being held, hearing my name
thrown, thrown like a rope from a very old pier
                        to hold me.

I want to catch the last echoes, reel them in
like a curing-song in the creel of my ear
                        to hold me.

I want Rodolfo to sing, flooding the gods,
Ah, Mimi! as if I were her and he, here,
                        to hold me.

Ghazal: Lilies of the Valley

Everywhere we walked we saw lilies of the valley.
Every time we stopped were more lilies of the valley.

Umbrellas passed – fathers, sons,
holding out a hand that bore lilies of the valley.

Every citizen of France
bearing through his own front door lilies of the valley.

But we were out of the know,
though reluctant to ignore lilies of the valley.

Our first May Day in Paris,
knowing nothing of folklore lilies of the valley.

Of Jenny Cook and Chabrol's
buttonhole the night he wore lilies of the valley.

He who sang *Viens poupoule, viens!*
and started the fashion for lilies of the valley.

How fashion then conferred, free
on *les ouvriers* at Dior, lilies of the valley.

Mais nous, sacré bleu, who knew
of charmed *muguets des bois* or lilies of the valley?

And though I wore the perfume
I have always worn before – lilies of the valley

– Diorissimo that is,
no one whispered, 'Meem, *j'adore* lilies of the valley'.

No one made false promises.
And if France did, who blames poor lilies of the valley?

Ghazal: It's Heartache

When you wake to jitters every day, it's heartache.
Ignore it, explore it, either way it's heartache.

Youth's a map you can never refold,
from Yokohama to Hudson Bay, it's heartache.

Follow the piper, lost on the road,
whistle the tune that led him astray: it's heartache.

Stop at the roadside, name each flower,
the loveliness that will always stay: it's heartache.

Why do nightingales sing in the dark?
Ask the *radif*, it will only say 'it's heartache'.

Let *khalvati*, 'a quiet retreat',
close my ghazal and heal as it may its heartache.

Ghazal: Of Ghazals

Ah sweetheart, you have sent me a book of ghazals.
You have sent me a bough and a brook of ghazals.

*I have even become tears to live
in your eyes.* Let me live in their look of ghazals.

Shahid is dead, great poets dying,
but his swansong is hung on the hook of ghazals.

May the rarest editions of love
bring us both to a shop with a nook of ghazals.

If love's too dear, Mimi, then wander,
penniless, in a long empty souk of ghazals.

Love in an English August

Twice I've gone as far as the High Street phone.
For no good reason. But to rein in passion.
August in London. Making time my own.
For while sun comes and goes, love is on ration,

lying open to the weather, on heat,
on hold. And I was never one for half-
way houses, never did learn to compete
with mild-mannered sisters, cope with rebuff,

temper quarrels with jokes. Freak storms with sighs
like small rain when drought's at the door. False comfort
to borrow heat from the sun when sun lies
under leaf, heat under cold. 'Temperate'

let's call it, for it cuts both ways, this trope
to prove even a full sun brings false hope.

To prove even a full sun brings false hope,
largesse earns little thanks, recall a cot
we broke, you mended, badly, as if rope
could hold together sleep as delicate

as that, a corner cupboard, big red cushions,
yellow mugs, the colour and history
two people meeting late in life might fashion
a new life with, leftovers of a party

the other wasn't party to till later
in the kitchen, when salad's at its best,
telling it how it really was, they savour
rich pickings, scrape the trifle bowl and test

the water, breakages, take out the trash.
For no good reason. But to rein in passion.

For no good reason, but to rein in passion
or rather, give it free rein, for without it
how can I swing goodbyes, stroll from the station
late at night under trees and sing about it,

how can I not 'concentrate on you'?
Perhaps, like that letter I wrote from school
about a fancy dress party, it's true:
to win a prize all you need do is truly

'consantrait'. I never knew – I've just looked it
up – I was going as a wedding cake.
And you, marking your one Lottery ticket
do, I recall, pause, concentrate. Good luck.

And keep it. My share I mean. Strictly on loan.
August in London. Making time my own.

August in London. Making time my own.
So quick to tell me everybody steals it
and I let them, where are you thief? Don't groan.
Own up. Where's my life, what thicket conceals it,

where've you put a decade and more, my prime,
my time with the children out of my hair,
over the hill and far away, that chime
of my maligned spinsterhood? Is it there,

under those papers, books you never read
or, tired of good intentions, pitched like tents,
dropped out of diaries, left lying in bed
with clothes? Come clean thief, where? And where's the sense

in playing for time? Here, sign the confession.
For while sun comes and goes, love is on ration.

For while sun comes and goes, love is on ration?
Can paupers then imagine, when sun's nailed
to the spot, rimmed round with fire, that creation
might decree free rations at least till sun's sailed

out of sight? No chance. So don't hold a glass
up to sky. Love's chained to a rock, come rain,
come shine, and heartache's been put out to grass.
But if sun's nailed to the spot and love chained

to a rock, then each in the mirror sees
what I see: who I was, became, am now.
Double-locked. Three skylights opened to tease
my menagerie of moths. Some huge, some slow,

too slow for me. Their wingbeat for my heartbeat.
Lying open to the weather, on heat.

Lying open to the weather, on heat,
on Hackney Downs, accompanied by Dante
and Love, his 'gaze on the ground', with *La Vita
Nuova* blurred by sky, I'm near where we lay

that once… but you wilt. Sigh. Abbreviate
my name, short as it is, hitch up your glasses,
rub your eyes, gaze into space as if fate
had called from a long way off and impasses

were all you had to go by. Love, so at ease
with bluffs, why don't you revisit a side road,
from a whole lawn pick one of poetry's
old standbys: dandelion clocks I showed you

how to tell time by. Blow. There's still a half-puff
on hold. And I was never one for half.

On hold. And I was never one for half-
etched outlines, loose holds on reality,
but with wingtips skimming grass and its rough
nap pricking shins, wind in my hair, with every

circle they describe, head-high, birds go through me.
Weave passages through flesh and blood, a rush
and throb of beat and swoop, a brush to groom me.
Groom me for vanishing in the clear plush

of air, flesh and fell, absorbed by the sheer
drive of it. And I, my own drives on hold,
who thought I could always steer on course, veer,
take leave of my senses, give in. To cold

winds from your halfway, your when-can-we-meet?-
way houses. Never did learn to compete.

...way houses. Never did learn to compete...
might be a fragment unscrabbled from sand,
torn and stained, heeled in from untrammelled feet,
from a stone where an ode, elastic band

were once balled around it; a message sea
spewed, a bad dog chewed and salt or saliva
made the first word run, the last bleed and me
mad about it. For I'm no deepsea diver

to fish unfathomable meanings nor
a mermaid wed to their beds where old seadogs
get wrecked, snore an eternity and more
and she too dumb to kick them, stick those hogs,

make no bones about it. I just get tough
with mild-mannered sisters, cope with rebuff.

With mild-mannered sisters, cope with rebuff,
With sweet serenity, keep your mouth shut
And when charity moans 'nothing's enough
For love, true love', give up those fags, you slut.

Called you a slut once, remember? Of course
you do. Wouldn't even bother to answer
the question. So why is it such a source
of embarrassment to me, yours? Mine never

was to you, was it? Of course it was? Oh.
Forcing me to kiss with a mouth rinsed out
with ashes, was that lust? Hardly think so.
Don't like to think what that was all about.

Thought I'd sing a song. Try it on for size.
Temper quarrels with jokes. Freak storms with sighs...

Temper quarrels with jokes. Freak storms with sighs.
That's no song. That's a dirge, mirthless and dour,
'defeated' you'd prefer. And I, loath to rise
to the bait of your defeat being ours,

ours mine, would give nothing away. No use
crying 'when's my turn to be given to,
given to first?' when someone who'll refuse
you nothing, nothing spare, is driven to

give in the ways he can, and can't, and won't
deny he's failed. I wish you had. Wish I
had allowed you to, asked for less, said 'don't
feel that way'. But you did. I didn't. Why

bolt the stable door? Feed self-pity? Covet,
like small rain when drought's at the door, false comfort?

Like small rain when drought's at the door, false comfort
pocks my sleep and I ache, dowsed with the feel
of you, you and you and you, to stay anchored,
moored to black rivers, grounded on the keel

of dream rows unresolved. Dream men, you motley
crew, shape-shifters who slip the hold of nightmare,
shiver in a shaft of motes, ghosts, I'll shortly
have you. But daylight brooks no see-through nightwear,

limbs in limbo. Daylight melts you. Like smells
you could swear you've scrubbed of all trace and can't
understand why they're still in your face, bells
that keep ringing after they've stopped, you'll rant

and rave, finally cave in. Dumb disguise
to borrow heat from the sun when sun lies.

To borrow heat from the sun when sun lies
in your voice, spring from the air when larks sing
at your approach, blush from a peach when fruitflies
buzz as you unload, shyly, everything

money could buy, I'd like, you'll cook, and one
wholenut bar I'd wish were bigger if only
I were smaller, is to belie the sun,
moon, flowers, trees, birds and bees, ads for lonely

hearts I read, secretly, and you don't. Don't
make me do all the wrong things now, like long
to love you. Don't turn my views back to front,
undo my vows, break my heart; leave it strong

enough for being, when sun's desperate
under leaf, heat under cold, 'temperate'.

Under leaf, heat – under cold, 'temperate'
skies now intemperate and glowering
with storms – takes the last of the sun, irate
with gnats, mosquitoes, chainsaws. Flowering

ramblers wilt on walls. England is at peace.
Your country, tiny island, devastated.
Mine, no news. Darling, we are refugees
from love, nurture, nature. And implicated

is our own, so unable to sustain
what is alien, intractable, fuse
colours of a flag into alltime rainbows.
Why not raise the white then? Let's call a truce.

Hand out blessings. Play archbishops and popes.
Let's call it, for it cuts both ways, this trope.

Let's call it, for it cuts both ways, this trope,
this bluff, this marriage of true minds, sly two-way
mirror, bending-the-truth-twice telescope.
Star to ships that pass in the night, a blue bay

that sparkles, green havens, earth's heavens, scrub
them all out, redraw, rewrite them. But this time,
each to his own, don't share them. Only trouble
is, won't they look the same, find the same rhyme

for thee and thine, rivers of wine and maidens'
veils so fine you can see not only limbs move
but marrow through them? For how many heavens
make one, which is the one on earth but love?

And love's not one to – oh grope for it, grope –
to prove even a full sun brings false hope.

To prove even a full sun brings false hope
how many times, when it blazed, did we cling
to shade, pronounce its grey, slippery slope
as safe and flames, homespun, poor candled things

the merest breath can snuff, as passions breath
inflames. Hatred, revulsion, rage. How many
flares did we scorn, each spark a shibboleth?
Prove me wrong. Show me an ear of corn, any

golden thing that grows, any vine tomato
religiously watered, courageously
staked on a windowsill and swear that no
fire, no faith inspired it. Outrageously

prove me wrong. This once. But go it alone.
Twice I've gone as far as the High Street phone.

Ghazal: Who'd Argue?

If I said every tear, each sob, each sigh
quietens, stops and all our tears soon dry,
                            who'd argue?

If I said every voice stung to the cry
'What is the point?' doesn't want a reply,
                            who'd argue?

If I said time will tell, heal, steal, fly –
take it, give it, do with it as you're done by,
                            who'd argue?

But if hopelessness did, who would deny
its right to be heard, if hope were to try,
                            who'd argue?

Who'd argue over love? Who'd follow my
example? You, my love? Then who am I
                            to argue?

Just to Say

I miss you – let me count the ways –
morning, noon and night;
I miss you on my darkest days
and when things for once go right.

I miss you in the inbetweens,
in shades of grey and gaps,
like bowling-alleys miss their greens,
lost mariners their maps.

I miss you like the tide its mark,
a church its congregation,
Londoners a place to park,
refugees their nation.

My old mistrust gives up the ghost,
my new misfortunes don't,
I miss the boat, the bank, the last post,
the film, the joke, the point.

I'm a misfit in my own skin,
a fist without a glove,
a bow without a violin,
an amoeba in love.

Counting pebbles on the shore,
I'm splitting hairs much finer
to mount up ways I miss you more
than all the tea in China.

I'm Christmas without mistletoe,
a firework missing fire,
so lost without my Romeo
I'd settle for the friar.

Yes, a misbegotten mismatch,
a score without a song
for a good-time girl in a bad patch,
a ding without a dong.

I missed my chance, I threw away
the line and missed my cue
the day you rang me just to say
miss you, miss you, miss you...

Song

I have landed
as if on the wing
of a small plane.

It is a song I have
landed on that barely
feels my weight.

Sky is thick with wishes.
Regrets fall down
like rain.

Visit me.
I am always in
even when the place

looks empty,
even though the locks
are changed.

Don't Ask Me, Love, for that First Love

after Faiz Ahmed Faiz

Don't think I haven't changed. Who said
absence makes the heart grow fonder?
Though I watch the sunset redden
every day, days don't grow longer.

There are many kinds of silence,
none more radiant than the sun's.
Sun is silent in our presence,
unlike love, silent when it's gone.

I thought that every spring was you,
every blossom, every bud;
that summer had little to do
but follow, singing in my blood.

How wrong I was. What had summer
to do with sorrow in full spate?
Every rosebush, every flower
I passed, stood at a stranger's gate.

Weaving through our towns, centuries
of raw silk, brocade and velvet
have swilled the streets in blood. Bodies,
ripe with sores in lanes and markets,

are paying with their lives. But I
had little time for the world's wars,
love was war enough. In your sky,
your eyes, were all my falling stars.

Don't ask me, though I wish you would
and I know you won't, for more tears.
Why build a dam at Sefid Rud
if not to water land for years?

Though we'll never see the olives,
ricefields, shelter in an alcove
from the sun, in our time, our lives
have more to answer to than love.

On Lines from Paul Gauguin

How do you see this tree? Is it really green?
Use green then, the most beautiful green on your palette.
And the gold of their bodies God made to be seen?
Make love to that gold and make it a habit.

Use green then, the most beautiful green on your palette
to shadow the world always chained to your feet.
Make love to that gold and make it a habit
to leave love eternally incomplete.

To shadow the world always chained to your feet,
don't be afraid of your most brilliant blues.
To leave love eternally incomplete,
nothing shines more than the love you will lose.

Don't be afraid of your most brilliant blues.
At night phosphorescences bloom like flowers.
Nothing shines more than the love you will lose –
these are lovers' bouquets with miraculous powers.

At night phosphorescences bloom like flowers,
like spirits of the dead in a Maori sky.
These are lovers' bouquets with miraculous powers
where all the colours of the spectrum die.

Like spirits of the dead in a Maori sky
with one eye on lust, one on disease
where all the colours of the spectrum die,
paint, blind Paul, your flowers and trees.

With one eye on lust, one on disease
and the gold of their bodies God made to be seen,
paint, blind Paul, your flowers and trees.
How do you see this tree? Is it really green?

Ghazal: The Candles of the Chestnut Trees

I pictured them in the dark at night –
              the candles of the chestnut trees.
Their name alone made them self-ignite –
              the candles of the chestnut trees.

I pictured them in the pouring rain
as they really are, pink-tinged on white –
              the candles of the chestnut trees.

How many there are and each the same!
same shape and colour, angle, height –
              the candles of the chestnut trees.

Seen from below, most unseen,
they throw no shadow, cast no light –
              the candles of the chestnut trees.

I saw how distance matters more
than nearness, clearness, to see upright
              the candles of the chestnut trees.

Inspired by 'Christ the apple tree',
I looked for a figure to recite
              the candles of the chestnut trees.

Lacking faith, I could do no more
than find a refrain to underwrite
              the candles of the chestnut trees.

As May drew on, the more I saw,
the more they lost that first delight –
              the candles of the chestnut trees.

I've searched for sameness all my life
but Mimi, nothing's the same despite
              the candles of the chestnut trees.

The Mediterranean of the Mind

i.m. Michael Donaghy

It's not just the heat and sunlight
I love so much in this landscape
as the whiteness of the ground,

glare of limestone, occasional
shells among stone and rubble,
ground feeling lighter than sky

as though heaven were already
here, and real, and detailed.
White dust rims my toenails.

The peaks of the far mountains
are so thick in mist one can't tell
if they are flat-topped or belled.

Villagers, in their mind's eye, supply
the missing crowns, their true shapes,
and cockerels points of the compass.

Everywhere else, death is an end.
Death comes, and they draw the curtains.
Not in Spain. In Spain they open them.

Many Spaniards live indoors until the day
they die and are taken out into the sunlight.
The duende does not come at all

unless he sees that death is possible.
The duende must know beforehand
that he can serenade death's house

and rock those branches we all wear,
branches that do not have,
will never have, any consolation.

★

Playing at house is divine.
What would one do with handfuls
of lavender picked on the hill?

I like the mixture of frugality
and generosity both of the village
and landscape. Lemons have spilled

to circle their trunks and wild
pomegranates silhouette crags.
Small and profuse, white figs,

ripe when they're splitting their skin,
are there for the reaching and
almonds galore that refuse to crack.

Fresh limes too and persimmons,
green on the tree, with the callow bloom
that will still be on them when they're red

and people ill-informed in the ways
of persimmons will eat them,
thinking they're ripe, and pull a face.

They are vessels for jam and properly
eaten only when the vessel's skin
is thin as glass and as clear.

The local delicacy is *turrón*,
'a blending of sugar, almonds,
orange blossom, eggwhite and honey

from bees that have dined solely
on rosemary'. Though how they
police the bees I've no idea.

★

As you'd expect, the morning
was quiet as a church, the doors
and windows shuttered, not a dog barked,

cock crowed, nor did the earth-shaking
tractors (usually one man and his dog
sitting on the hood), trundling

up the Carrer de la Mare del Miracle
under my window, pass. Even
the weather knew it was Sunday,

being chilly and overcast. Then,
as though someone had turned on
a radio at full blast but even more

immediate and loud (I thought
it was upstairs in the little apartment),
a brass band burst into full song.

I rushed to the window in time
to see a small group of followers
vanish round a corner and shortly after

they came again, on the other side,
this time preceded by a band of stout
women in turquoise shirts who handed out

leaflets to the women in doorways,
stopping to chat and laugh. Meanwhile
the musicians stayed tantalisingly out of sight.

Later, I saw a thin girl in red Lycra
with her clarinet and clip-on score
going, I assumed, home for lunch.

★

How joyful the sudden music was.
The whole village sprang to life.
Here, on the quiet mountainside,

I feel like a child, dependent on doors
and windows – or in this case, pines –
for a glimpse of shining brass.

Like flying above a hometown,
knowing your own house is somewhere
down there or passing it by train

behind all the familiar landmarks.
Seaside music without the sea.
Seaside music in a small Catholic

mountain village down in the heart
of the valley and the sound
rising to the very mountaintops.

Earlier in the week, I was listening
to the builders just behind the villa.
For every blow of the hammer,

an echo, more sound than echo
so clear it was, answered back
and where the echo struck

behind the sierra, I imagined
an invisible pueblo growing nail
by nail as the hammer fell

and the echoes nailed them flat.
But the fancy is never as inventive
as reality with its brass bands.

★

Tonight, a gecko is silhouetted
inside the glass of a streetlamp,
every small alternate stepping

magnified as he patrols the pane,
the bulb so fierce and close
it's a wonder he doesn't burn

while outside, circling the lamp,
a bat caught in the light. Today
a *langosta*, camouflaged in greys

on the cane of a lounger, so still
even its antennae were visible,
yet alive. Now crickets are trilling

the seconds, the pulses of night.
Chris talks about Michael
as we sit at the kitchen table.

Michael reciting 'Ode to Melancholy'
and Yeats. Michael and Ruairi
going down to the almond grove,

their voices drifting up from below.
Michael crossing the room, strangely
often, to hug Maddy on the sofa,

how patient he was with Ruairi,
how steeped he was in Lorca.
On the last night, during supper

on the terrace, fetching his flute,
how he played and when everyone
stopped talking, urged them to carry on.

★

Constantly struck by the abundance
of fruit rotten on the branch
or ground: figs trodden underfoot,

kumquats blackened to tar,
whole verges heaped with carob.
The trees themselves sapped of life.

You wouldn't starve here, living
in the wild. But you might die
of thirst, so dry is everything

on the outside but inside, nurturing
juice – thousands of prickly pears
tumbling in swags down hillsides.

You seldom see anyone working
in the fields, save for the little
fearsomely noisy tractors winding

along the terraces. Black lemons,
shrivelled to the size of walnuts,
smell twice as lemony, caramelised.

Occasionally you see a newly planted
rose looking false and out of place
but the fields are covered in a host

of rusted flowerheads and the butterflies
too are rust, orange and brown.
The great burnout happens in June

but in April and May, there's
always the almond blossom
and as early as January, wildflowers.

★

My eyes find it hard to focus –
is it the light? The dramatic rise
and fall of mountains, *barranca*,

the near and far? And my ears
assailed with buzzings and dronings –
even the trees, with barely a breeze,

rattle their pods. I have umpteen
bites. Bites, sunburn, a surface of
innumerable itches and underneath

a sadness for the land and its people,
many of them old and disabled,
leaning on the arms of daughters

who sing as they crawl, arm in arm,
up and down the one street
every day at the same time.

I move quietly through my rooms,
wash fruit and hardly talk
to anyone. *Hola!* I say quickly

to everyone I pass, sometimes
so synchronised with their replies
or mine to their greeting, it sounds like

the same voice, without overlap
or counterpoint, just the one
Hola! between two strangers,

I being usually the younger,
though the children too playing
on doorsteps say hello as I pass.

★

I was mentally tracing the path:
follow the wall – a strange
butter-yellow painted balustrade –

to reach Carrer del Calvari
where the wall gives way to a sudden
very steep flight of steps in sandstone,

on one side planted – and drip-fed
through thin black plastic tubing –
with indigenous and imported shrubs.

The Carrer del Calvari is a white
zig-zag path laid along the cut
of terraces, bordered with pines

and, at intervals, wayside shrines.
Inset, on glazed tiles, the soldiers'
faces often obliterated and gouged,

are the XIV stations of the cross.
My 'study', as I call it, lies beyond
this path in the yard of an abandoned

café under the old Arab fortress
where the children's pool is hidden
by ivy, padlocked, and corrugated iron

makes ticking noises in the heat
like rain; where Spanish fir, Aleppo pines
smell sweet and aromatic, cones

on the topmost branches still fierce
and clinging on, even on those trees
whose spurs are blown away and dead.

★

Everything is quickened by knowing
how short my time is here,
how easily I'll forget it, how

different it will be should I return.
I struggle with the names for things
and even were I to learn them,

whatever the language might be,
they wouldn't evoke – except for me
perhaps – themselves. Today

I have a visitor to my 'study',
an old gentleman in shirtsleeves
who asks how it goes and tells me,

in Valenciano and mime, bunching
his fingers and motioning them
in his mouth, it's time for lunch.

Very Cézanne the whole landscape –
you sense the presence of brushstrokes,
round-headed and flat, almost

the palette knife. But I'd place my words
behind the surface, weaving through nouns,
the undifferentiated but various pines,

into a Mediterranean of the mind
where, like the white *ermita*
culminating in open ground,

some white and holy destination
hoves into view and at the foot of it
one looks, not up, but out.

★

Ermita Sant Albert
is always locked, its tarnished
bell chained and silent.

I look through a small dark pane
like a porthole set in the doors
and cup hands round my eyes

to telescope the dark. A plain,
spartan interior: cloistered arches;
a niche with stucco cherubs, a lace

tablecloth and at Christ's left foot,
a large bunch of dried flowers
jutting out from the shelf; in front,

a table also with a cloth, a picture
and other devotional paraphernalia.
Nothing else. But the big church

in the village square, forever
clanging its bells – heard in London
if you use the public phone –

is fronted by benches and orange trees
where groups of old men sit and,
on market days, middle-aged women.

The padre has been renamed Juan.
He's a refugee from Rwanda
and much loved by everyone.

The side doors are currently a gruesome
shade of brown. It's the undercoat,
we overhear him say at Pepe's.

★

Sitting in the last strip of sun
setting behind the Moorish ruin
I am, having spent all day at the pool,

glad of the breeze and shade.
This is the time I normally leave.
Now, I come to take my leave

of my 'study', the sun, this week
outside my life and the last heat
before the dreaded winter.

Smoke's rising from a bonfire
and through it, the olive terraces
look charred, trunks black and leafless.

The surface I'm beginning to penetrate
seems prickly and sour, despite
a generator's hum, jasmine at the gate,

the old tragic pines with young ones
at their feet, newly planted in rows
with rather unpromising oleanders.

Sounds are isolated in the quiet
much as the trees are in barren soil.
It's not they that grow naturally

out of the soil but the ochre
houses, tile-roofed, earth colour.
I could weep for the flies and the dog

who seems to be barking at his own
bewilderment. But to weep
is to own, is an act of presumption.

★

I do not think any great artist
works in a fever. One returns
from inspiration as from a foreign country.

Every artist climbs each step
in the tower of his perfection
by fighting his duende, not his angel

nor his muse. This distinction
is fundamental. The angel dazzles,
but he flies high over a man's head.

The muse dictates and sometimes
prompts. The muse and angel
come from without; the angel

gives lights, and the muse gives forms.
But one must awaken the duende
in the remotest mansions of the blood.

I'd like to be here in the dark
and look down on the lights of Relleu
rather than up at the floodlit chapel.

Even the stars last night were suspect.
Stars where no stars are, and lightless.
But the moon was bright and legitimate.

I'd like to write with my eyes closed,
blurred as they are with oil.
Behind my lids today at the pool,

I saw the sun as one green light
like a green persimmon. Angel fruit.
A green sun like a green apple.

The Middle Tone

Seldom do we Andalusians notice the 'middle tone'.
An Andalusian either shouts at the stars or
kisses the red dust of the road. The middle tone
does not exist for him; he sleeps right through it.
                              Federico García Lorca

Just so I spend my life asleep.
Stars, if there are, might shine above
and dust, dust that I've always loved's
now dirt at most I lightly sweep.

But *cantaor*, I too exist.
My middle tone of dung and nectar,
flower and carrion, is a star
that fell, dust I too once kissed.

On a Line from Forough Farrokhzad

It had rained that day. It had primed a world
with gold, pure gold, wheatfield, stubble and hill.
It had limned the hills as a painter would,
an amateur painter, but the hills were real.

It had painted a village lemon and straw,
all shadow and angles, cockerel, goats and sheep.
It had scattered their noises, bleats and blahs,
raising a cloud, a white dog chasing a jeep.

It had travelled through amber, ochre, dust
and dust the premise of everything gold,
dust the promise of green. Green there was
but in the face of a sun no leaf could shield.

It had rained that day. It was previous,
previous as wind to seed. O wild seed,
as these words proved: 'The wind will carry us'
– *bad ma ra khahad bord* – and it did.

Scorpion-grass

I travel with groundsel, ragwort, poppy,
seed anywhere and don't look back.
Let any wind sow me, any rough patch be
my home between the cracks.

Forget-me-not call me – if only, if only
memory grew in my tracks.
I blow at a window, away on a balcony,
kick my heels down a cul-de-sac.

The child who stoops to examine me
– my cymes, my sign of the zodiac –
will see, for every star in the galaxy,
there's one in the broken tarmac.

Give me a bombsite, wasteground, masonry,
history I'd otherwise lack.
Shallow my roots but how instinctively
I live without rooting for facts.

Facts are a bind and biography
a woodsman wielding an axe.
Don't give me a plot or a family tree
but a garden swing, a throwback.

I travel with groundsel, ragwort, poppy,
seed anywhere and don't look back.
Let any wind sow me, any rough patch be
my home between the cracks.

The Meanest Flower

i

April opens the year with the first vowel,
opens it this year for my sixtieth.
Truth to tell, I'm ashamed what a child I am,
still so ignorant, so immune to facts.

There's nothing I love more than childhood, childhood
in viyella, scarved in a white babushka,
frowning and impenetrable. Childhood,
swing your little bandy legs, take no notice

of worldliness. Courtiers mass around you –
old women all. This is your fat kingdom. The world
has given you rosebuds, painted on your headboard.

Measure the space between, a finger-span,
an open hand among roses, tip to tip,
a walking hand between them. None is open.

ii

Cup your face as the sepals cup the flower.
Squarely perched, on the last ridge of a ploughed field,
burn your knuckles into your cheeks to leave
two rosy welts, just as your elbows leave

two round red roses on your knees through gingham.
How pale the corn is, how black your eyes, white
the whites of them. This is a gesture of safety,
of happiness. This is a way of sitting

your body will remember: every time
you lean forward into the heart of chatter,
feeling the space behind your back, the furrow

where the cushions are, on your right, your mother,
on your left, your daughter; feeling your fists
push up your cheeks, your thighs, like a man's, wide open.

iii

The nursery chair is pink and yellow, the table
is pink and yellow, the bed, the walls, the curtains.
The fascia, a child's hand-breadth, is guava pink,
glossy and lickable. It forms a band

like the equator round the table. The equator
runs down the chair-arm under your arm, the equator
is also vertical. The yellow's not yellow
but cream, buttery, there's too much of it

for hands as small as yours, arms as short,
to encompass. Let tables not defeat me,
surfaces I can't keep clean, tracts of yellow

that isn't yellow but something in between
mother and me be assimilable.
Colours keep the line to memory open.

iv

Here where they're head-high, as tall as you, will do.
This is the garden in the garden. Here
where they're wild and thin and scraggy but profuse
such as those ones there, these ones here, no one

looking, no one within a mile, you'll find
flowers to pick and to press but before their death
at your hands, such small deaths they make of death
a nonsense and so many who would notice?

with the best ones, flat ones, left till last, take time
to take in the garden, the distance from the paths,
the steps and the terrace crunching underfoot.

Soon you'll hear a whistle. The garden is timeless.
Time is in the refuse, recent, delinquent.
Go as you came, leaving it out in the open.

CHILD: NEW AND SELECTED POEMS

As if they were family, flowers surround you.
As if they were a story-book, they speak.
They speak through eyes and strange configurations
on their faces, markings on petals, whiskers,

mouth-holes and pointed teeth. They are related
to wind. Wind is a kind of godfather, high up
in the branches. They're willing you to listen
to them, not him. Even now you're too old

– though too young in reality for most things –
to understand their language. Once, you could.
You can feel the burn in the back of your mind,

as you hold their gaze, where the meanings are,
too far away to reach. What creature is it
that can stand its ground, keep its mind so open?

There are stars to accompany you by day.
After you've gone to bed, they fall to earth
like dew but, to accommodate that dew,
presumably fall first. You've seen the fluff

from your blanket, a blue cloud in the air;
hooded in your cloak with its scarlet lining,
walking between the pine trees late at night
seen stardust so fine you took it for granted

or took it for vapour, mist, a kind of mistake –
the way a sleeve rubs chalk along the blackboard
and the numbers smudge, x's disappear.

Well then – you've only to turn a midnight sky
upside down to show, when they close above,
the stars below of chickweed, speedwell, open.

vii

The pink primrose flower's an aberration,
a nail discoloured, blood clot on a yolk,
a cuckoo in the nest. How did it get there?
You'd like to pull it out, out from the clump,

beak it like a worm. This time it's an odd one
but sometimes the whole clump goes red as if
some shadow had passed over and instead of
letting it pass, the blooms had taken on

the stain themselves. The yellow ones are true
registers of light and shade but the pink ones,
no matter how bright the sunshine, far away

an overhanging hedge, can never change.
They carry the shade inside them, their veins are blue
and your blood runs cold to see they too can open.

viii

Because you are a child, the earth's dimensions,
of which you know so little, rise to greet you.
Walls, albeit with peepholes into orchards
long abandoned, may be too high to scale

but who would want to scale them when scale itself
and a wall risen up like earth at eye-level
have appointed you like Gulliver to dwarf
the already miniature: ivy-leaved toadflax

mimicking waterfalls, curtaining caves?
The same insect cities you'd see in grass
you now see in stone without bending, stooping,

and your spine is a wall itself. For this,
you are thankful: earth's horizontal shelves
standing, like a glass museum case, open.

ix

These are the things you have made or have yet to make:
six knitted egg-cosies, a sailboat in cross-stitch,
the coronation coach replete with its team
of horses painstakingly cut out and glued,

an apron, a book of miserably pressed flowers,
countless milk bottle top pompoms, embroidered
handkerchiefs and one darned for Janet Blue,
all of them neatly and the last passionately.

But materials are intractable
whereas spelling, grammar, punctuation,
bend to the curve of your thought and your thought,

brighter than any needle, magnetised
to their rule, kneels to their rule: a knight errant,
lifting his visor as the Queen's casements open.

x

You're not the centre of the universe
nor do you wish to be. The very thought
fuels your fear of fire, of Joan of Arc
terrifyingly bald, burnt at the stake.

You'd prefer death by invisibility
and diminution, death by camouflage
in florals. You don't think of dying, however,
hovering on the edge of being noticed,

organdie sleeves perked like butterfly wings,
your antennae alert. In later life
you will home in on fields of tiny flowers,

an infant's fading kaftan pinned to the wall,
Annette in an orange shawl, linings, borders,
bindings and trims, each dot, each floweret open.

There was always that familiar ache:
finding your own spot under the trees to read,
the heart always gravitating to love,
still smarting from the last humiliation.

There was coconut ice in pink and white,
between sugar and spice, time to apportion.
You were always fair. When it came to tears,
however, you were mean, a veritable

Scrooge, a Shylock crying out for his jewels
while all the monkeys in the wilderness
scattered and scrambled, gesticulating wildly,

until the savannah, the whole plain, was bare.
What *were* the thoughts that lay too deep for tears?
Oh monkey-child, it's time to lay them open.

I think of Wordsworth's hermit in the woods,
that shrivelling in the heart that leads one deep
into solitude, the longing for it,
as if life were not already too lonely

and a grandchild learning to shred a catkin,
as you once did, no more to be cherished
than her catkin stems. I am entrusted with them:
in one hand, balled, a nest of rusted tails,

in the other, stripped stalks I'll gratefully
chuck from the train. Poetry's on the run.
From exhaustion, the inability

to imagine a larger world and one
too sick to be hurt into words. Be kind,
sweet April, you with your mouth, first vowel, open.

NEW AND
UNCOLLECTED POEMS

Iowa Daybook

Two men are rolling tables,
round tables like golden discs,
one golden arc of circles

on the amphitheatre's strip.
Now they wait, the tables,
the round golden masks

and the sky says nothing.
Now the white canoes
and the three white geese.

Now they peck in tandem
while an insect calls from among
the trees. Where are the gods

of Iowa? The 'drowsy ones',
'he who paints pictures',
'dust-in-the faces'?

A day so grey. I did my laundry.
There was nowhere I wished to go.
Whatever pain I had left behind

was better left. I switched on
all the lights in my room, all
the reading lamps and ceiling lights

and still the day was grey.
I will go quietly to the bookshop
and hear what the poets say.

The river feels the rain before we do,
rain-rings quickening to signal it.
All the many trees of Iowa

– Norway Spruce and White Pine,
Cottonwood and Maple,
Linden and Sycamore –

are as nothing to this tree of light,
rainlight, shimmering
an arrow across the river

and the sky leans down to say,
'I am the tree their shadows create,
fallen that you may see me,

shining that you may float,
oars still, moving me in your wake
as the wind moves spruce and cedar.'

How lovely to lie flat on the ground,
trees overhead and birds I can only see
because I'm underneath them.

Like fish, their bellies are pale
to camouflage them against the sky
and their backs dark to mimic earth.

Last night we saw a praying mantis
scaling a wall, a plain thing,
inches long, more stick than insect.

This is a landscape made for
woodcuts, carvings, patchwork quilts,
cornfields thrown like doormats

on distant hills. Fields and roads follow
the old grid pattern for homesteading.
Let the home-hunting immigrant

be informed that a free home awaits him
in Iowa, the Waterloo Courier proclaimed
two decades after a troupe of 14 Iowa

had sailed to Europe to perform
tableaux vivants in George Catlin's
Indian Gallery, the venture ending

when Little Wolf's wife and child died,
and a decade after the Republican Party
was founded in Iowa City in 1856.

England, London, I am
homesick for you. My little
local streets, messy and human,

cafés where I can sit and smoke,
each so close to the other.
Homesick for the small-scale,

the crooked, the left-alone.
I sit among trees, old and young,
in the lobby of a landscape.

Every road is made for dapple.
Shadow can be as shadow
was meant to be – lovelier

for being grey. The precinct
is a flood of dapple that lends
itself to smells – kerosene, coffee –

in every city of the world.
We walk in the cast of mind
that dapple gives us. Nothing,

not even the bright acacia,
is lovelier than the ground itself.
And now that our lovemaking

has accepted failure and limitation,
how gently we lie together, asking
for nothing, giving sleep permission.

Why have I never been in love?
Singing in the shower, washing
my voice in water, spray.

And the woods – I miss the woods,
someone says, and hearing him
we see him as if he *were*

the woods he has vanished in
and love is like that too,
a wood we cannot search.

The Amish, like the Mennonites,
are pacifists but, unlike them,
they practice shunning. We pass

the water tower, schoolhouse,
the windmill and cider press,
a birdhouse for purple martens,

the chicken house for 8,500 hens,
clothing centre that fixes buttons, zips,
sends bales to third world countries,

the Sunday School where services
are held in German, the silo,
Jo's welding shop, brother-in-law

Simon T's quality horses,
grandpa houses, the coffinmaker's
yard and the new Kalona library.

The cardigan was in blue, wool shades
of blue like a Fair Isle knit but
so finely done I knew I couldn't afford it.

Bizarrely, the names of America's ten
most dangerous men were woven in it,
men who had murdered somebody

close to me in my dream. I buy the rainhat
I've been looking for. *I see unknown places,
I let myself slide down the slope of dreams.*

Emily Dickinson sat in her room
and the galaxy unrolled beneath her feet...
She sat in her room and the garden

and the orchard outside her windows
took on the ghostly garments of infinity...
There are poets of the dark and deep.

Not all of us can go there.
Depths were never truths I reached.
More, the quiet monotony I never

thought of as monotony
but peace. Nothing I loved more
than making torn things whole.

I never looked to be healed.
Torn rather, torn open,
to prove I too could feel.

Oh to be a better reader,
a patient one, steadfast
and young enough to know

years of reading lie in wait.
To live with Dante, say,
months at a time, to live,

tracing a finger from side to side
across the trough of an open book,
bilingually with Hafez!

The song must come from elsewhere,
from some other organ. The word
'organic' was first used by Aristotle

to refer to parts of warships – parts
of a whole that made the whole thing work.
(Suspended between the giant spokes

of the wooden starboard paddlewheel
as it turned on display were two spiderwebs,
one a perfect diagram, one half-rent.)

Why am I awake? I have climbed
out of the pit of sleep, out of the river
itself. Foghorns call over Iowa.

'Here is the place', 'beautiful land',
in all its spellings: Ay-u-vois, Ayavois,
Ay-u-ou-ez, Aiaoua, Ayoüs, Ayoës, Ioway.

These were never journeys
that we planned, travelling
on boats that tipped us in the wind

though the lake was calm
and fish, if fish there were,
yes there were, those three or four

you pointed out, calling, fish,
there are fish here! had faded
out of fish and into memory's hair.

It was when I learned as a child
the word for 'yesterday' in English
– and what an odd word it was –

that the underside of all my words
was suddenly revealed. Nouns
I had secured with gravity and string

levitated; furniture grew wings;
every chair I had sat on, bridge
I had crossed, called me to account:

where were you, who were you with?
(An Iowa student changing my sheets
is an art teacher at the local Montessori

where the kids have a globe covered
with sandpaper so all the continents
feel rough, he says, smoothing the slip.)

Yes. The earth is flat, like a lost
floating board… and I remember
little tasks of pleasure, how the world

lies flat on my ironing-board, warm
to my palm, while my children
sleep upstairs. What have we sacrificed

to come here? Jamby, whose mother
died only weeks ago, whose mother
became transparent in a sunset.

People cling to each other
but no one has the strength
to be the branch – we are leaves

now, nothing but leaves.
Choi, from South Korea, who says
her language is useless, useless,

who has spent her time translating it;
Genti, struggling out of Albania's
fifty years of isolation; 'Doc',

Ashur from Libya, who tells me
my poems are all the same; Srijato,
sad to have his young wife leave;

and Choi again, stepping off
the path, saying in her useless
language she likes the sound of leaves.

Dusk and everything comes closer.
Iowa's first Baptist Church,
its gabled roof under the maple,

four flights of shallow steps,
moving with small blind windows
towards poetry it can hear

in another language, another age,
in fly-over country as Emmanuel
reads at Shambaugh House, comes closer.

'It is what bears our name'
Chief No Heart said when he
and Moving Rain presented it,

a map to back their land claims,
before the Indian Commissioner
in Washington D.C.

Big Sioux and Little Sioux,
Niobrara and Rock, Raccoon
and Skunk, Cedar and Turkey,

once rivers that were torrents,
run-offs from glaciers piling land
at our feet – here they are in charcoal

like a forked branch outside
my window, meeting at the junction
of the Mississippi and Missouri.

A false fire alarm in the night.
We stand, shipwrecked on the grass,
islanded without our things.

To say island is to invoke
bells ringing, people missing,
to name, like Adam, all your things.

And since the island is ageless,
time is told, if told at all, only
when the lyric spreads her wings.

I move bench, following the sun.
The candle of the sun is enclosed
in a copper cylinder casting

shadows along the ground
much like the filigree of trees.
But the filigree is that of letters,

each perforated scroll of which,
illuminated at night, projects
headlines on the Adler Building

in an indecipherable script.
'They will be able to read
what I wrote, but what I wrote

is a mystery itself' the chandler
said to the CIA who cracked the code
of a light sculpture similar to this.

I too have been a candle
filtering languages. Why else
would I sit, on the first morning

of wintertime, in a courtyard
outside the School of Journalism
& Mass Communication building,

if not to escape the cacophony,
the babel of other languages
I can't hear silence in?

The Streets of La Roue

From the red house on the fish quays
where the old harbour was, the plane trees
and the cobbles, in Wednesday drizzle
when thought travels on diagonals, colour
is pure and unlascivious, take the metro
from Sainte Catherine, via Jacques Brel
and Saint Guidon on the Erasmus Line
to Anderlecht – Anderlecht being, myth says,
a rough translation of 'the love of Erasmus' –
to find yourself between places, languages,
on the outer ring between city and countryside
where roads abruptly give way to fields, cows,
in a garden city whose streets commemorate
the aspirations of its founders and its people.

La Roue is on the outer ring. La Roue
could have been a blacksmith's wheel,
La Roue could have been a torturer's wheel:
spin it – *roue, roue, roue,* in a backstreet,
a hoop and a stick and here come the twenties,
a little bruiser in his grey shorts, grey shirt.
Here come the pavements, double crocodile
of nuns with their charges, the tramlines, river,
the lake where the children bathed. Here
come the houses, big ones, little ones, four
small wooden ones in a block that in fire
would burn. Here come the Belgian, French,
the Spanish and Portuguese and here come
the old who were born and still live here.

Like an old film star, the lone magnolia
is in flower but this is not Sunset Boulevard,
this is *Droits de l'Homme*, boasting mailboxes
in metal, wood, tin, most like birdhouses
with two tiny dormer windows looking out,
perplexed. Where is the postman? Where
are the addressees? *Attention au Chien!*
C'est moi qui monte la garde ici! But
what does he guard? The cherub urns,
barbecues, slides and trikes, basketball posts,
looking up and barking, the number plaques?
What need for number when each doorway
is marked by its own carefully chosen tree tile,
wall bracket, weathervane, carriage lamp?

On Rue de l'Émancipation, parked in a white van,
Façade Express undertakes the cleaning of facades.
But nothing is what it seems. Under the asphalt
run the old tramlines, under the tramlines, damned
for all its sewage to run eternally underground,
what might have been a tourists' caféside river.
But for all the builders' rubble, plastic bags,
piping, wires, breeze-blocks, tiling, planks
and paving stones, there are giant brussel sprouts
vying with camellias, geraniums and compost
sitting beside the pebbledash, japonica flowering,
rhododendron and broom and in a window,
behind the yellow primulas, a black and white cat,
black-nosed with a soot mark, looking anxious.

From No. 4, particularly pretty with an espaliered
peach tree, climbing rose on a three-way arch,
the sound of running water, a windchime
and an awning still bearing traces of artificial
Christmas snow, a lady opens her window to ask,
Vous cherchez quelqu'un? I am looking
for La Roue, I am looking for its guiding spirit,
where will I find it, *chez vous, chez vous,*
chez eux? Look, here is a bench for poets
and the elderly, a crescent where daisies grow
freely on the verge, *Place Ernest S'Jonghers*
overlooked by an orange crane and tremendous
sudden drumming from some den or loft
where a teenager drives them all berserk.

But let us praise folly, for 'He who loves
vehemently no longer lives in himself
but in what he loves...', Erasmus says,
and no more so than on *Rue du Symbole*,
where a young girl in a tracksuit is pulling
on a pink string a toddler on a trike, sucking
a dummy, surveying the world; a grandma
in a long brown robe and hejab accompanies
a gaggle of Moroccan schoolkids; an old spruce
wears a wild afro of ivy; a baby stone rabbit
nibbles at weeds and on net curtains, embroidered,
spreads an idyll of ponies, pastures, windmills
and turtledoves flying out of their cages to flirt.

CHILD: NEW AND SELECTED POEMS

'The more perfect the love, the greater
the madness', Erasmus concludes in his praise
of folly. And folly it is, surely, to come upon
an open space in the *Rue des Colombophiles*
where, beyond a fence of corrugated iron strips,
car panels, wire fencing, is a flat area of allotments,
well dug but empty of produce save for a few
yellow mustard flowers and some far greenery.
Back gardens flaunt chickens and daffodils,
a fine cedar fronting a row of poplars, the chimneys
of the concrete factory, the railway bridge, trains
going to Ghent and, over the fence at the bottom end
of the allotments, helmeted cyclists gliding past
on the canalside like ducks in a shooting gallery.

Doves cooing on the *Rue des Huit Heures*
bring you to the *Plaine des Loisirs*. Pleasure,
more folly. Sun sets above the black plane trees
and on a bench this time, *ALO MAMAN,*
Je t'aime Valentin, are messages from Kelly.
A young one in her mother's arms, stretching out
a baby arm, is calling repeatedly like the dove,
'da-ddy, da-ddy'. Grass is littered with daisies
and the long thin diagonal shadows of the trees
underline the white lines the daisies scribble
like shadow-writing. A blade of a boy in a black suit
with a black dog yanks on the lead, making the dog
snarl and twist and half-leap as if on circus training.
The glittering of the grass swells like waves at sea.

'…and his joy is in proportion to his withdrawal
from self and his preoccupation with what is
outside himself' our guiding spirit, for I believe
Erasmus himself has been invoked, continues,
'When the soul meditates on travelling without
this use of its limbs, this is certainly insanity.'
And suddenly Soul arrives at a basketball ground
and, not wishing to travel unfingered, unlimbed,
straddles a bench to carve a soulful message:
pour la vie mon bb, invoking the names
of Christel, Souliman, Ismael. Soul kicks
at broken sidelight glass, plastic fork tines
scattered in the dust of *Place Ministre Wauters*
and asks, 'Who once ate here under the elms?'

On the corner of *Rue de l'Énergie*,
you will find the boulangerie/fromagerie
of Tonton Garby. In a French beret
and moustache, Monsieur Tonton
(whose less energetic brother serves
alternate days in a seven-day week)
holds forth in English, in French.
He has lived here for 43 years,
travelled all over – Oxford Street,
Piccadilly Circus, America (here
he bursts into an American accent)
and once, with his family, to Sri Lanka.
'Come on,' he cried, 'let's do the elephant tour!
Everything, everything!' And so they did.

We've come full circle back to *Place de la Roue*
but this time behind the church, once too small,
now, rebuilt, too big. After all, it's only a moderate
garden city, swelling with immigrants' kids:
these two girls, one with bad eyesight and glasses,
both with long brown ringlets, bright blue rollerblades,
legs splayed like young deer finding their legs;
this tubby boy, pushing his sister, *Vite, vite!*
Two boys bending to their mothers' headscarved
brows with kisses. And the young Moslem women,
laughing, handling the baby in the pram as lightly,
with as little concern as their mothers before them did.
This little girl in plum, standing a foot away, swinging
her arms violently from side to side like a windmill.

'A glutton for letters', Erasmus said of himself,
his humanism trying to unite, above the confusion
of beliefs and races, all the clerics who desired
not to betray the cause of the spirit. In his house
lie a cast of his cranium, fragments of his coffin.
In the Room of Rhetoric, a statue of him stands,
the saint holding back his torn entrails, armed with
carpenter's tools and hoe, square and compass.
In profile, sharpened quill in hand, studied hands
on an open book, fingers ringed, he sits writing.
He wears three coats, so cold were the winters,
and the black hat from which he was never parted.
Outside, leaf ponds float his adages – UBI BENE,
IBI PATRIA, brass letters half-submerged, rusting.

Afterword

for Archie

Today I adjust
the favourite wall
of a lover.

The vine it supports
won't arbour us
as promised.

The old arrangement
looks odd to others,
to us;

looks like another
country
we must have known.

E.A. Markham, 'A Life'

Not in my heart do I carry you
with me everywhere
since your death, but in my mind

have you accompany me –
pedestrian and passenger,
side by side on the top deck

or standing while I sit
when there's only a seat
for one of us on trains.

Not in my heart but in my mind
beside me, talking, while I
gaze out through a mist of green

as I have always sat with your absence.
Even the rain is green in London,
so much green in May.

★

I have but recently arrived, am,
in fact, arriving. I look to the right
to see if the tide is coming in or out,

to the left to see the mountains
disappearing. I have settled in
but the horizon is departing.

How can one imagine a person
in death without his lifelong feelings:
the shame, the pride, the lifelong

cover-ups and disguises, sudden
jolt of eyes without their glasses?
No one was here to meet me.

I can come and go like the cats
under the tables with only
the odd face turned toward me.

★

At the depth of my shins and calves,
a pale green filter, deepening
to the height of the pelvis, creates

a bridge to the deepening blue
of L'Outro bay, at first aquamarine,
then turquoise, then pewter blue,

then way out there where the hills
become like Chinese hills, hardly real,
the rulered royal blue of the horizon.

The green filter creates an aquarium
for stones, the large ones green as if
a layer of algae were swaying over them.

There are zigzag lightning lights in the water
and then, where the cold will hit my belly
and breasts, the lightnings disappear.

★

Of your body what is left
but ash and a single hair?
A perfect ring, one coiled spring

of microscopic wire.
Archie, you are gone now.
Gone, gone, gone. Gone utterly,

irrevocably, yes, you are.
Look how solid our buildings are,
how material the sky.

Paris is where you left it,
so am I.
I, small as a single hair,

the infinite divisible.
You the indivisible nowhere,
whole, entire.

★

Mid-afternoon when snorkellers,
knowing the sea has warmed sufficiently
for their old age, take to the waves,

so the waves too, for those who lie
listening with their eyes closed,
come like dolphins out to play –

their swishes and flurries creating
fish-shaped sounds to play across
our ears. Beside mine I place a shell,

a glint of mother of pearl on its whorl,
and think of that one last stray black curl
clinging to a tile back home for weeks,

months maybe, after your death.
The last bath I took, cleaning
the bath beforehand, washed it away.

★

There was a wall or kind of cupboard
and, caught between the louvres,
the elbow of a shirt I recognised

in the language of dream-recognitions
as my son's and I leapt on it as I would
a drowning child and, grasping some corner

of the shirt or sleeve, dragged it out
in one great slash from between the slats.
Last night a small boy slipped perilously near

the edge of the quay and his young mother
leapt from her chair to yell at him, pointing
at the dark night water, and I wondered

at anger and the fearsome tenderness
it springs from, the fear and helplessness
despite all our warnings and harangues.

★

Was it twice or three times
I woke from a nightmare?
Each nightmare twinned

to the one before, one
brother to the other.
Nothing is yet forgiven.

A sickness rises in me.
I will take it with me
on the long drive home

for I have nothing else to take –
no ring box, no sarong.
When I think of the word 'sickness'

childhood calls to be born again,
this time in the open air
with an open mouth.

★

However long I listen to birdsong,
I distinguish neither vowel nor consonant
and therefore can't describe it in words

though the rhythm does persist
like the rhythm of persistence itself.
And so you, being dead, are like birdsong

and the rhythm that persists is the afterword,
he's dead, he's dead, he's dead.
On one side of me at the beach today

were Italians, on the other, French.
And I revised my opinion of the French,
both the people and the language, finding them

charming, the fat women and the thin men.
(Only because you, who loved the French,
are dead.) Death has altered me too late.

★

There is a step up to the shower-closet –
the showerhead is blocked and I wash,
sluice myself half-squatting under the tap.

Through the shutters I see the back
of the chair on the balcony spread
like a fan. There is a ceiling fan.

My blanket is very soft at night, even
against my face. In the fridge are
half a melon, seeded, some apricots,

the last of a small pot of honey
and a knife. Wind bangs the door
at night even though it is locked.

I light a last cigarette. The nights
are black. Everything in my room
is white, including my pencil.

★

I'm surrounded by the wild furniture
of Crete – boulders, light tan and grey,
cushions of sage, trees, chandeliered,

forming a pool of shadow beside the church,
a window on a choppy turquoise sea.
Yet I'm drawn to the long bare stone table,

speckled where the whitewash has eroded,
a bench for the solitary and arthritic.
A poem should be a makeshift thing,

Bishop said, and the spirit too needs
furniture to invite it in – otherwise
where would it be, lost on a headland

of heat and wind, nothing in its hands
to carry home, no home but a windy church
with a banging door, a music of wind and tin?

★

Imagine a corpse laid out on a hill.
Imagine a hillside with a goat
grazing halfway up it; the bell;

the wind; the difficulty, when a wind
blows really hard, of seeing.
But the sound rises; at one point,

almost sounds like singing.
There'd be birds circling, surely.
Here there are no birds – the odd seagull,

tilting in and out of visibility.
There'd be wolves, hyenas, jackals.
A quiet, concentrated tearing.

And a loping away to their young,
a red around the mouth like her sheep,
Louie was telling us, who love beet.

★

Yiorgos, you haven't fixed my shower yet
but every morning you glide to my table soundlessly
to bring me coffee with a deference I don't deserve.

If I thank you in Greek, you smile. After a year
you have cut your beard. Now you bring us brandy and cakes,
wheat, nuts and honey, for it's the one year anniversary

of your brother's death. Your mother, old now and heavy,
helped me carry my case up the steps. It was heavy
with paper and books and too many clothes to wear.

I was here last year as you remembered, clasping
my hand in yours, warmly in greeting. During the year,
now and then I thought of you sitting in your chair,

the long sea-gaze in your eyes. Man of few words,
here are a few for you: *efkaristo, kalimera, kalispera,*
and the silence that lies between them of a long sad year.

Night Sounds

I can hear myself moving around
    in the dark. My footsteps
  lagging up the stairs. Now
I am quiet, listening to the light
    that strikes the plant in
  leaves of light at the turn.

An animal in the brush, large
    enough to encompass a shuffle
  here, a footfall there. Ooh.
I am lovely in my sounds.
    I am moonlight and darkness,
  death and habitation.

I thrill to the sounds my memory hears.
    Sounds I have made in my life
  through all my life – a child's hand reaching
for water, chink of the glass
    replaced. They moon about
  the house, free to help themselves.

They do. How bright it is
    in the fridge! You can hardly
  bear such brightness. But where am I
between this soft thud
    and the next? I am in all rooms,
  on all stairs, lumbering and animal,

enough to make you worry
    when a door clicks and I, on this side
  or on that, forget myself. Hear that?
What? Nothing, I hear nothing.
    Only the pillow crackling,
  a rasp, a whistle of breath.

River Sounding

For six weeks the river has been brought
into dry dock – like the ark with its animals
on board – six weeks to tell its story.

Live feeds, hydrophones, accelerometers,
have cast a spell to subdue, to set adream,
bring audiences to listen, languages

in young mouths aflame with travel.
Our eyelids droop. We long for sleep, to lie
like Gulliver in long grass, eyes like pools

for rainclouds to traverse. The whistle buoys
are probes in our ears. Their story doesn't reach us,
drowsy in the white noise of the fountains.

We are all eyes, not ears. We like to watch
the pigeons, iridescence on their ruffs,
going about their business; the fat lady,

lifting her sari, paddling in the fountains.
We are impatient, too impatient to hear stories,
too sceptical of history, too eager to connect.

There might have been music from the barn,
animal grunts on the other side of the fence
or a barely discernible suck as I drew on a cigarette.

I could hear nothing from the goosehouse and the silence
that lay over the fields, distant copse, and far away
over the sea itself, was a silence you could smell.

It smelt of frost and dung, nicotine in my hair.
A young couple, sitting on stools outside a cottage
in Connemara, would remember it for years.

My own partner, dead now, more than two years dead,
had no inkling of it, tapping ferociously on his old
manual typewriter and I, leaning on the fence,

hearing the silence but without an inkling
of the years, painful, diminishing, that lay ahead,
would hear it doubled, trebled, one silence

crouched within another, whenever I lay in bed,
the radio on like conversation under the sea,
as I pulled the duvet up and over my ears.

Through it all, the drone, the whine.
Foghorns, whistle buoys, bells that clang together
from the four points of the compass,

sink into silence as you raise your head
to listen: that one note, mechanical
and lonely, orphaned from the river.

The fountains become meadow, become grass.
Kneel to their own feet, lift and rise like
glass jelly fish on stems. Sounds at my back –

call and response, chatter, consolation.
Untethered sounds with nowhere to go
but into the void, calling out their –

'I am bull, I am horn, I am herd.'
The animals are lowing in their stalls.
The lonely buoy, the long-necked bell.

'Wish-wish' the fountains go. 'Over here,
over here' go the bells. 'John!'
the big clock strikes. 'Jim, Jim!'

the little ones say. 'The experience
being out of control' a voice butts in,
signing off to a darling on the other end.

Without my love, there is no song.
Without my love, no silence.
A carousel without a pole,
two apple halves without a whole,
no centre, no circumference.

Without him, the idea of him,
desire draws up its blanket.
Stars come out and look about,
a halfway moon gives way to doubt
with no one here to thank it.

Ears grow deaf, eyes grow dim,
and why is the street so long?
The best is over, you know it is,
for he took your best and made it his
inimitable song.

Without my love, there is no song, etc.

The shadow of Seamen's Hall, crowned
by five gilded urns, guards sunlight
from the lightwells. Who would forego

the light of the courtyard, jet grove
of fountains, for the dungeon damp,
cobbled dark of the passageways?

My dead would never come here.
People of sand and sunlight, people
of snow and mountains. Who are these dead,

collective dead, poets so love to write of?
My dead were never collective, were
as singular as they were in life, touching

all four points of the compass, homeless
as these bells. Their names won't thread
on a string, and too few of them for chains.

Down in the catacombs, the walls are made
of water, but not sweet domestic water
to cup in palms, sluice in public baths –

no, underworld water, rivers of dream
and nightmare, rivers of sons and daughters.
My living dead cling to their curtained rooms,

dim corridors, wedged open doors to parlours.
But the dead come one by one: each has
a stanza in the heart, each an echo chamber.

I have heard two voices in the river,
one of the singer, one of the listener
and both were the voices of poetry.

One was a daughter and one a son,
one would listen as the other ran on
and both could do either equally.

Where one was blind, the other was dumb,
when one of them wept, the other grew numb,
changing place simultaneously.

I have felt two terrors in my heart.
If one fell silent, the other would start
but it was the silent one that broke me.

Time stepped in to heal the breach
till both of my terrors were out of reach
and I returned to normality.

But the river ran on, I knew it was there
in the either/or, the when and where,
hiding, dividing, mercilessly.

Enter the warmth of the Dead House,
green subaqueous light, soft planking
underfoot, piped rumblings overhead.

Turbines, beam engines, flex their muscle,
lagged iron, steel, lift ten-ton weights.
The coal bunkers are utterly silent,

blacked in, set back in brick pilasters.
What do they know of water, ambient
memories of river? Steel cables

are all they know of sky, slow roar
of the city, trundling above on giant rails.
We ourselves are the drums, arteries,

hollows through which the sounds vibrate.
There is nothing inside the Dead House.
What is inside, inside the rust-stained walls,

trapped, enormous, are the unfathomable
languages of water. Nothing to do here
but feel. Listen. Choose to forget.

I never remember my dreams.
I wake exhausted from them.

And when I do it feels like
I'm wearing a skin inches thick –

glutinous and alien. I never remember
my dreams for I'm not who I am in them,

what bred them. God forbid
I should write, then read them

through the glass of a vivarium
when I could be out in the sun!

I'm not answerable to the dark.
Let others sing the snake.

For a tidy soul, one who relishes balance
and, above all, symmetry, to be pencilled in
at a corner of this courtyard is to inhabit

nothing so much as an architectural drawing.
Shadows under arches cross-hatched, banded
masonry, pediments, lintels, balustraded

parapets punctuating rooflines, become
two-dimensional, perfect in perspective.
But into the frame, like a princess in a story,

runs a young girl through the fountains, sparkles
on her dress and sash pink, silver, green.
She squeals, she streams; her father in city clothes

holding ready a large white handkerchief,
her grandfather in the shade reading a leaflet
in his quiet greys and signet rings.

Not the bells, whistle buoy in the distance,
fountains sparkling in the sun, but an Indian
lunchtime outing has served to make us real.

I barely cried. When my father died,
and my grandfather before him,
when I heard the news, I smiled.

Some force pulling up the corners
of my mouth so irresistibly
it was all I could do not to laugh.

Some people cry for months, even if
they live abroad, the more so for not
being there, for the guilt, anger, love.

As far as death goes, I'm a child.
With a child's curiosity, I wonder
what they look like. 'Like an angel',

they said of him who was no angel,
'clean as a baby, not a mark'.
I remember the soles of his feet, my Dad,

pumiced and soft. The safety pin
he pinned to the lower end of his sheet
for fear it would touch his mouth.

Today sympathy is our watchword. Sympathy
and symmetry, a line of sun and shadow cutting us
into perfect halves at 5pm the clock confirms.

And dividing the blue above, a vapour trail,
long as the courtyard's wide, driving its parallels.
Granite glints, silver water throws clouds of spray –

great silver fans of diamond. Pigeons burble
contentedly, sun warms the wool of our coats,
settles on a cheek or two to burn. Strawberry red,

red as cherry pulp are the pigeon's three spread talons.
Up and over it climbs the iron strut of the chair.
Could it be drums at play, softly in the lightwells?

The river winding up for the day, packing away
its instruments? And the bell calls, lucidly in silence.
A woman is wearing a rose, two of them in her hair.

Cretan Cures

As well as blue eyes to ward off the evil eye,
you may also find *filahta* pinned to the back
of a small child's coat or discreetly tucked away

in a grandmother's layers. *Filahta* are most commonly
gold medals of the saints, sachets filled with basil,
pieces of olive branch, candle shavings from an altar.

As for me, I've crossed the water under a starlit sky,
stars falling around me like jangling charms on a bracelet.
I've looked up at the stars, seen sevens and eights

– wishbones, tents – a sky of Arabic numerals.
I've searched for blue, blue of the bay, among pebbles.
Green I find, muted, and every possible shade of grey.

I hold a handful of the cool ones that have slept
in shade. They're like skin, I think, so we lie
on the beach holding hands, me and the pebbles.

During the power cut, I step out on the terrace
to check on the stars, now shorn of light pollution.
The tavernas have never been so noisy, so excited,

like children playing hide and seek in the dark.
But when the lights come back on at 3am,
while we lie thick and drugged with seaside sleep,

still the tables have to be cleared. A silent army
in the night collecting cutlery, bottles, glasses,
threading braziers where coals grow cold and ashen.

Should you be suffering from a summer cold or sniffles,
grate onions for a poultice on your chest, grind them
with Ouzo into a paste for swollen wrists or ankles.

Garlic is also good. Dangle a braid above your door,
carry a clove of it somewhere on your person.
A single clove grown into a head is best, but rare.

In the narrow shade of the seawall, cats, lined up
like china ornaments, sit gazing seaward. It's not sea
they're gazing at, it's Nikos on his fishing boat,

untangling fish from his heap of nets piled up
like yellow seaweed beside a white plastic bucket
into which he plops the good ones, throws cast-offs

to the cats on the quay who eat, one eye open.
Fish are wise and knowledgeable. Revere them
for their silence. And never throw bread away.

Instead, throw it to the chickens, pigs, dogs even.
Bread must be consumed by some living creature,
it would be a sin to throw it away. 'Verona' lists:

still the gunny sack on deck is full. Nikos
scratches his head, sets to, slipping his hand
through a hole, braceletted for a moment in gold net.

Among us, Hazel is a nurse – luckily for Jean
who slipped in the shower and gashed her arm
to the ulna. Jean's eyes are round blue cornflowers.

I use perfume on mosquito bites, hoping to quieten them.
The fridge is empty of cherries now – I've washed
the plastic tray. How soothing plastic is, and melamine,

on holiday. I provide my own room service, stand
on a chair to slip the curtain rod back into the finial
(to see my skirt-length I have to stand on the bed).

If someone pays you a compliment, remember to say
Skorda (garlic) under your breath and spit three times;
ask them to spit on you too. Garlic doesn't smell

till peeled, so you can stick a clove of it in your bra.
Bat bones are also lucky (though killing bats is not),
so if you find one, slip a fragment into your purse.

Hazel is wearing a straw bonnet, Macmillan daffodils
and a blue enamelled butterfly clustering at the back.
Henry's hat sports an orange bandanna, two butterfly pins

in two shades of blue, but essentially they are dressed
in beige. Are they married? How well they sleep!
Well, together. Well-travelled as people steeped

in their own roots often are – 'We survived', she says.
Their breakfast table is a small cluttered island and they
two kindly weather fronts holding it between them.

Hazel, don't hand him a knife. Let him pick it up himself
or there'll be crosswinds later. And never, on any account,
empty your account. Money begets money, remember.

And when the crow caws, say *Sto kalo, sto kalo,*
kala nea na me feris – go well into the day, crow,
bring me good news! Crows anywhere spell disaster.

The cat sleeps soundly as a carpet. Flies don't wake her.
She sleeps like a crescent moon, horned moon, tabby moon
under the taverna's awning. Slip off your sandals now

and lay them down the right way up, upturned shoes
spell death. If the soles by chance fall facing up,
turn them over immediately, side by side, say *Skorda*

and a spit or two won't hurt. Now that you've taken
so many precautions, you're bound to be safe and well.
Now that you're closing your eyes, you still see light,

an eyelid edged with it, and your cheeks rising up
like a rock of shadow, double-humped, below them.
And when you open them, how doubly bright the water!

Ellie, with her sight restored thanks to laser surgery –
after a lifetime of seeing in a blur, how doubly bright the sea
for her! (and Marmite helps with her loss of taste and smell).

The Poet's House

for Robert vas Dias

The poet's house gestures towards a roof
and a chimney aslant the lemon grove
raised on the first of the bancales which climb
the mountainside towards a daylight moon.
It's like Waller's dark cottage of the soul,
dark inside but facing the rising sun
blind-eyed and its rusted ironwork balcony
with room enough for the old poet to stand,
early mornings, sipping coffee, hoping,
hoping today for a visit from the muse.

Pigeons roost in the rafters and the night wind
would bang the door, hanging on its hinges,
were it not wedged by long grasses and rubble.
The poet's house is for viewing across a valley
where it guards the view. Barely a love nest,
set square against a landscape – harsh maybe,
but softened by olives, pomegranate trees,
scrub dotting the lower terraces and the walls
weathered, bleached, remembering in their plaster
gouges and pocks the soft pale colour of frescoes.

No smoke from the chimney, no floor for a bed,
but something cosy as a cottage loaf
the way it nests: a square with a sense of rondure.
Does it hear the quietness of the morning
or is it, being centuries old, stone deaf?
A poet's house that was never built for song,
not for talk or companionship, for wine
or laughter. And its balcony too small
to sit there reading as the sun moves over.
Set at the foot of a slope, commands no vista.

Negatives, absences, withdrawals, withholdings,
under its red-tiled roof, hold conference.
For the soul is nothing if not negative –
look how its furniture has been abstracted,
it is all shell, shell, shell, the seed of a dwelling,
husk of an old migration. We long to possess it.
We dream of bright conversions, enough to make it
habitable: a floor, a stair, a shower;
a garden but no fence, for the goats, the dogs,
would be welcome; a riot of tumbling flowers.

But when night descends, the poet's house
is illumined by a borrowed moon, by floodlight
from the castle. Inside, nothing is illumined.
Remove its shell and it would stand, a Mecca,
Kaaba, for the soul to circle, but not
with the eye, the ear, a groping hand
or tentative step, only with the passage
of the whole body, being, the self's dissolve,
for without dissolve, there is no emergence.
Were it in my gift, Robert, I'd ask you to stay.

Come and sit here with me on the old stone wall,
half wall, half rubble. Let the sun beat down
with the sound of running water way down
below in the gulley and a visible breeze
blowing the oat grass, the very thought of breeze,
to cool us. We should have sat by the pool but no,
here we are, ringed with the sound of cicadas
in a central well of silence. Insects hum,
nose-dive past, leaving a nervousness behind them.
Come, let's brave the door. Or at least its shade.

Slip into the cool now. Sit quietly
on a blue rush seat chair, framed by cobwebs,
a timber plank with a row of rusted nailheads
and two wooden poles to prop the splintered
roof beam overhead. Once, the house was painted
in pastels, Edwardian pastels, childlike patterns
on the walls in faded greens, blues, ochres.
A staircase leads out of sight and plaster, brickwork,
stripped bare, reveal an ocean underneath
of shell striations, fish eyes, land mass shapes.

I've left the door ajar, dragged vines in, greening
at their tips, it's so cool and quiet in here,
tiles underfoot covered in leaves, stalks, dirt.
Don't worry, nobody will ever come.
Even the animals, strewing droppings
along the path, know to keep away.
There's nowhere to move to, only the eye
can travel, seeing nothing but ruin, naming
nothing but ruin and the ear that listens,
through the door, for unfamiliar birds.

Look back on where you were, across the valley,
the middle distance arid, melancholy,
drawing the heart towards it, straight on a sightline
towards this buckling roof, red gentle slope,
the balcony door half-open like a mind
in two minds whether to penetrate or drift
around an elevation like a face.
The poet's house looks steadily beyond,
towards the object of its own desire,
knowing its own mind which is also gentle.

And so it stares in stasis, blank and immune
to interruption, a stand against forgetting,
the loss of where we were. A hermit's dwelling.
And in place of electricity, plumbing,
there's the steady hum of cicadas, sawings,
whirrings and buzzings, a whistling stream of sound
like gas jets hissing: its mechanical life
is without, not within. Within, on diagonals
spiders walk, spins a gaping hole of thought,
waiting for a poet to come and think it.

A Tree of Heaven, *Ailanthus altissima*,
grows near the house, its canopy bowed down
with clusters of samaras turning pink.
Sun longs to enter. Making little forays
across the grass, hanging little flags
of light along the trees. Shadows are misty
now and the face of 'Casa Fenollar'
watchful as if to call the shadows in
from where they hang precipitously by handholds
down the ravine or in the depths of branches.

But it does not call. It trusts to the campo
till, in time, of their own accord the shadows
thicken at the door and the fingers of sun
let go, sliding off the guttering.
Vast the vistas are but the casa looks
only to its own patch for it's enough
to be so wakeful and so solid. Backlit,
the Tree of Heaven flutters, edged with gold,
but why talk of heaven? Right here on earth,
Trees of Heaven grow everywhere like weeds.

Notes

p. 14, **Earls Court**
Ah! Vieni, vieni!: from Giacomo Puccini's *Madama Butterfly*.

p. 18, **The Bowl**
 p. 19, *Chenar*: plane tree
 p. 19, *Lahaf-Doozee*: hawker's cry of the 'Quilt Man' who repairs quilts
 p. 21, *Sineh Sefid*: Mt. White Breast

p. 40, **Plant Care**
 p. 41, *Farangi*: foreigner
 p. 41, *Farsh Forooshi Ahmadian*: Ahmadian's Carpet Stall
 p. 41, *Befarmayid*: After you
 p. 41, *Ghalian*: hubble-bubble
 p. 42, *Bokhor*: Drink / eat

p. 59, **Tintinnabuli**
Quotation from *Arvo Pärt,* Paul Hillier (Oxford University Press, 1997).

p. 60, **Ghazal: The Children**
Salgado: Sebastião Salgado, Brazilian photographer and photojournalist.

p. 87, **Ghazal: To Hold Me**
Rodolfo: Mimi's poet-lover in Giacomo Puccini's *La Bohème*.

p. 89, **Ghazal: It's Heartache**
Radif: the refrain which follows the monorhyme in the ghazal.

p. 89, **Ghazal: Of Ghazals**
Quotation from Agha Shahid Ali's ghazal 'Of Water' in *Call Me Ishmael Tonight* (W.W. Norton, 2003).

p. 103, **The Mediterranean of the Mind**
Quotations from Federico García Lorca's lecture, *Play and Theory of the Duende.*

p. 115, **The Middle Tone**
Federico García Lorca epigraph from *Deep Song and Other Prose,* ed. and tr. Christopher Maurer (Marion Boyars, 1991).

p. 125, **Iowa Daybook**
p. 129, Quotation from Alberto Manguel, *With Borges* (Telegram Books, 2006).
p. 130, Quotation from Charles Wright, *Quarter Notes: Improvisations and Interiors* (University of Michigan Press, 1996).
p. 132, Quotation from Yehuda Amichai, 'Patriotic Songs', in *Amen* (Oxford Universiy Press, 1978).

p. 142, **Afterword**
E.A. Markham's epigraph, 'A Life', from *Looking Out, Looking In: New and Selected Poems* by E.A. Markham (Anvil Press Poetry, 2009).